Nine Lives

Nine Lives

Shun Mie Shee

iUniverse, Inc.
New York Lincoln Shanghai

Nine Lives

iUniverse books may be ordered through booksellers or by contacting:

iUniverse
2021 Pine Lake Road, Suite 100
Lincoln, NE 68512
www.iuniverse.com
1-800-Authors (1-800-288-4677)

Because of the dynamic nature of the Internet, any Web addresses or links contained in this book may have changed since publication and may no longer be valid.

The views expressed in this work are solely those of the author and do not necessarily reflect the views of the publisher, and the publisher hereby disclaims any responsibility for them.

ISBN: 978-0-595-46847-8 (pbk)
ISBN: 978-0-595-91139-4 (ebk)

Printed in the United States of America

Contents

Prologue

It's no wonder my Gina has had problems all her life.

I was born with problems, too.

My mom and dad had both grown up in orphanages and they had no education. We lived paycheck to paycheck and I could count all my mom's dresses and shoes on the fingers of one hand.

When I needed new clothes or if I needed a coat, I had to beg. All my friends had nice shoes and they even had dresses that matched their socks. I looked at myself and I looked at them and I would cry because I looked so different.

I didn't understand. I was too young.

I didn't know why God would test us all like that.

My mother would tell me things about money, but all I knew was that I wanted to look the same as the other girls.

My mother and father always argued, and I thought they argued because of me. Later on I understood that they only argued about money.

When I was little, I was afraid of my dad because he was always screaming at my mom. When he wasn't home, I'd play with my mom in the kitchen and help her put the dishes away and clean up. When he was home, I'd go into my room and close my door and lock it and not come out until my mom came up and got me.

My father worked long hours, but he didn't make much money.

I just wanted to grow up quickly so I could move out. Then I could be like everybody else, like all the other girls. I could get a job and I could buy my own clothes.

When I was in the seventh grade, I met Rob, the boy who would become my husband.

I was seventeen when he got me pregnant, so I never finished high school. I couldn't wait to get married and have our own home. I'd never have to hear my father come home and scream at my mom again.

We moved to his parents' house before we had enough money to get our own place.

Rob's father drank.

One evening I was home alone with his father and he told me to sit with him and have a drink. I poured myself a Coke and sat down next to him on the sofa.

"You're a very pretty girl," he said. "But do you ever think about what's going to happen to you from now on? You have no education. Neither does my son. You quit high school. He did too. All this time I worked and saved my money so my son could go to college, but now he'll have a family. He can't go to college. He'll have to work hard and long hours, just like me. It won't be easy for him. You've interrupted my son's life. He's just too young to get married. You're a little tramp and a whore and you're ruining my only son's life. You're not even married, but you're pregnant. You're just a tramp and a whore, you are."

I'll never forget what he said to me, getting drunker and drunker by the minute as he talked. My husband came home that night and I was crying and I told him I wanted to leave, but we had no money and I was pregnant.

My husband finally found a job and he started to work. He went back to high school in the daytime and worked at night. I had started working too. We saved our money.

I couldn't wait to leave that house either. I cried a lot and I was not myself. I kept asking my husband to go find our own apartment and he'd tell me he was trying.

We went to look at a one room apartment in the back of someone's house. It cost eighty dollars a month. We took it.

I was five months pregnant by then. I had started drinking on the sly.

Later my husband decided to join the service and I went away with him. Afterward we came back to Bridgeport, Connecticut, where we'd grown up. We both found jobs and we worked hard. I already had two boys and then I got pregnant again.

I had a baby girl and she was beautiful. She had blonde hair and blue eyes.
Gina.

We still lived in a little apartment. I couldn't wait to find a house so each of my three kids could have their own room. We went to the bank and took out a G.I. loan and we were able to build a house out in the country, in Derby, Connecticut.

Our marriage was wonderful then. We worked hard, but we had fun. Even though we still had hard times financially, it didn't seem hard then.

We had four bedrooms in the house and by the time we lived there for two years, we had all kinds of animals and pets because we had three acres of yard. We built a pool too.

My husband became friendly with one of our neighbors and they went out fishing a lot and played basketball a couple nights a week. They both started to drink when they were together.

Our marriage had already started to cool off and my husband was acting like he was single again, going out and partying with our neighbor.

My husband always called me from work to tell me what time he'd be home for dinner, but when he started hanging around with the neighbor, he forgot he had a family. He thought he was single and maybe because we got married so young—he was only eighteen—and because I was now twenty-four, a little over-weight and already had three kids, he began to feel like he missed some part of his life.

Even though he was beginning to drift apart from me, we still acted like husband and wife in front of the children.

One day he told me he was going over to play cards with our neighbor. My son suddenly got sick after my husband left and I called the neighbor's. In the background I could hear girls laughing and it sounded like a lot of other people there who were laughing too. I told him I needed him home and said I might have to take our sick boy to the emergency room.

He would not come home.

The kids were all young and I didn't feel I could take them all to the emergency room at the hospital. It was late at night. I felt my son's head and he no longer had so much of a fever so I gave him two more aspirin and we all went to bed.

After that I started to worry.

One day my husband stayed home from work. He was drinking and smoking grass. He asked me to try smoking some with him.

"It will relax you," he said to me.

I wouldn't touch it. I just went to my bed and started to cry. I drank.

After that, our relationship was never the same. We started to go in different directions. All I did was keep the house and take care of the kids. I paid the bills. I shopped for groceries. I didn't want to show the kids that there was something wrong between my husband and me. I tried to keep doing everything I had been doing before with no changes.

My life felt like the trials of Job.

Finally I couldn't stand it any more. I wanted to find out what Rob was doing. I went to his work one afternoon and hid outside, and when he came out, I followed him to someone's house. After a while, I went up and rang the bell.

A girl opened the door.

"Wait here," she said to me. "I'll call Rob for you." She went back inside and I heard her telling Rob there was somebody at the door who would like to see him.

He came out and pushed me back into the yard.

"What are you doing here?" he yelled.

"I was looking for you. You have to come home with me. I can't do everything myself."

"Never follow me again!" he yelled.

He was so angry he pushed me again and then punched me hard in the face.

I got back in the car and started to cry. I started driving, but I was crying so hard I could barely see the road with all my tears. I had to pull over and calm down.

My parents were home with the kids and were watching TV when I returned. I went into the kitchen and tried to wash off my face. I kept washing it with cold water, but when I looked in the mirror, I saw that my eyes were still red from crying and one was swollen from where my husband hit me. I wouldn't be able to hide it from my parents and children.

My mother took one look at me when I came out and asked me what was wrong.

I couldn't tell her. I said that I had fallen and hit my face on the ground. It was just an accident, I said to her.

"You don't have to tell me," my mother said, "but I don't want the kids to see you like that. You better go straight to bed and calm down. Have you eaten yet?"

"No," I said. "I can't eat. I'm not hungry." I think she knew I was in trouble.

My mother gently pushed me down the hallway and into my bedroom.

"I'll put the kids to bed," she said.

It was about this time, too, that my daughter Gina started to act up.

Gina was very pretty.

She had blond hair and blue eyes. She looked like she was fifteen when she was twelve because she had developed so fast. Her breasts already looked like those of an eighteen year old. I was worried about my two boys going after her so I let her move to my sister's.

My boys were always fighting and screaming. Gina was not comfortable with the two boys so I figured she'd be better off with my sister and her kids in Bridgeport.

I worked in the evening then and my husband worked in the day. We were both busy and I constantly had things to do. I didn't know until much later that my sister had let Gina go out with other kids in the evenings and sometimes she and her husband would smoke marijuana with Gina there at their own home.

One day, when Gina was visiting me, I went through her purse and found cigarettes. She was only twelve. I was upset. I asked her how long she'd been smoking and she said she got the cigarettes from her aunt. I started to worry about her. I thought she'd been safe with my sister because my sister was home more than I.

I was wrong.

One day a policeman called and said he'd picked up some kids drinking and smoking grass in the street. One was my Gina.

I had to go to the police station. The policeman explained the boys and girls had empty cans of beer and even some heavy liquor and they were sleeping. The officer thought they had grass too. The kids were all only thirteen or fourteen.

The other mothers were there at the police station getting their kids too. The police sent them all home with their parents.

I said to Gina that she had to come home with me. I wouldn't take her back to her aunt's. She told me, "No. I want to go either to my aunt's or grandma's house."

I asked her why she didn't want to come home.

"Just please don't take me home," she begged. "I won't do this again."

Only much later did she tell me her older brother had been beating and abusing her.

When she went to her grandma's house, her same friends from the street came and picked her up and they all still went out partying.

Gina's grandma would ask her what time she would come back and Gina would tell her in a couple of hours. Her couple hours would be way past midnight, though. Grandma told her she wasn't keeping her word.

Her grandma asked her what she did outside and Gina told her they went to the movies or they went to her friend's house to watch TV.

One night I went and followed her. She and her friends went to a gas station to hang out. I followed her further and they went to different gas stations and smoke grass.

That night I told Gina she had to come home with me and she did.

The next day she said she was going out.

She never came back. I couldn't find her anywhere even after I called the police to report her as missing.

Finally I called my sister and asked her if she knew where Gina was. She said she thought she might know because sometimes one boy came there to pick her up and he lived nearby. My sister said she would drive over there and see if Gina was with him and she would call me back later.

When my sister got to the house, Gina was there with Ruben, a boy she used to hang around with on the streets. He was a little older than she. My sister said she had to come home with her. Gina got her things and went with my sister.

After that she stayed at my sister's again.

My sister went to Gina's bedroom one night and Gina was not there. My sister called me and told me.

I went to Ruben's house and she was there. She didn't want to go home with me and she didn't want to go to her aunt's house. I didn't feel I could force her to do something she didn't want to do because if I did, she would never come home again. So I left her there. I couldn't tell her what to do. I knew she was a minor, but she wouldn't listen to me.

I told my husband about her, but at first he ignored me.

I didn't know where to turn to or who to talk to. I was lost. I didn't feel like I could communicate with anyone. I prayed to God, but didn't feel he could hear me. Maybe he wasn't even listening.

One night my husband came home and asked about Gina. I told him that she didn't want to come home and she didn't want to go to her aunt's. She was living with her boyfriend. She was barely fourteen.

Rob became furious. He'd been drinking, too.

He took his gun and went to her boyfriend's house. He knocked on the door, but they wouldn't answer so he forced it open and pointed the gun at Ruben. When he did, the gun accidentally went off.

Ruben's mother called the police and my husband was arrested. I had to go to the police station and bail him out.

That night Gina came home. I asked her if she knew what she was doing to us, to me especially. I told her she was too young to run away from home, too young to do any of these things. I said she was acting like she was twenty years old.

I looked closely at her face. Her teeth were yellow. She had dark circles under her eyes. Her fingernails were dirty. I kept asking her why she didn't want to come home.

She finally said to me that she hadn't wanted to tell me, but her brother had abused her. That's why she never wanted to come home.

We had been busy working and trying to pay the bills and we thought the kids would automatically watch themselves while they grew up. When they're small, kids are a small problem. When they grow big, they're a big problem.

I didn't know what to do. I was no longer myself. My husband was not cooperating. My daughter was giving me problems. One of my sons, Jimmy, was schizophrenic. I found out he'd been beaten so badly by my older son that he would often bleed from the nose. Now I had to watch him constantly and he had to take his pills so he would behave.

My problems were non-stop. If not with my daughter, with my son. If not with my son, with my husband. Why would God do this to me?

I was only thirty-five, but I looked like I was fifty-five. I couldn't eat. I couldn't sleep. I had gained weight. I had wrinkles in my face.

I couldn't control my daughter. She did what she wanted to do. I couldn't do anything with her, no matter how I talked to her or begged her not to do drugs or to drink.

She wouldn't listen.

So I stopped chasing her and my husband. I just let them do what they wanted to do.

I decided to leave it all in God's hands.

One night my phone rang, but I didn't pick it up. My husband wasn't home. It kept ringing and ringing and finally I went to answer it. It was a nurse at the emergency room of the hospital. She said they had my daughter. I put my clothes on and took my son with me.

Gina had started hanging around with a motorcycle gang and she would ride with them. They had all gone out partying that night and Gina had been on the back of a motorcycle that had run off the road and into a deep ditch.

The doctor told me she had broken ribs, a broken leg and, the worst, she had broken her neck. Her scalp and face had cuts all over them and were both black with stitches when I saw her.

She stayed in the hospital for a long time.

They had a detox facility in the back of the hospital. Gina had come to realize she was doing bad things to herself and she agreed to go into detox for close to two months, but her boyfriend Ruben came and brought her whatever street drugs she wanted while she was there.

She never dried out.

One night a nurse found Gina's drugs in the side of her bed. After that she couldn't have any visitors for a while and she got a little better.

Then Ruben came to the hospital in the middle of the night and picked her up and took her away. I couldn't tell my husband that she had run away with her boyfriend. I just said she wasn't in the hospital any more.

I was worried about her and I went back to her boyfriend's house. I knocked on the door and his mother came and opened it. She asked me to please come in and wanted to know if I wanted some coffee.

She told me Gina was a nice girl, and when she lived there, she helped her set the table and grocery shop, but no one could tell her what to do.

I told her that Gina had run away from the detox center without the doctor's okay and that I just wanted to know how she was doing.

Ruben's mother said she guessed Gina was okay. The stitches in her face had healed. She still limped a bit, and she thought that would take a long time to heal completely. She said she was sorry that Gina and I didn't get along.

I told the woman that I hadn't know that she had been drinking and smoking pot and that I thought her son had started her doing those things. She said she didn't know. She was busy. She had four kids. She worked.

I said, yeah, we're in the same boat.

I told her my husband and I were not getting along too well. She knew that, she said. Someday she said, she would tell me about her husband.

I told her she looked like she was a very strong woman.

"Sometimes," she said. "I pray to God a lot, too."

I told her I had to get going and she said she would have Gina call me when she came in.

I went to my sister's and knocked on the door. I was in tears.

My sister told me I was running around and around like a maniac and nothing was going to change. I should just let these people alone and let them do whatever they wanted to do.

"But I'm Gina's mother," I said "No matter what she does, I still have to care of her."

My sister just shook her head.

"Let her go," she said. 'You're running around like a chicken without her head and you aren't taking care of yourself. Without you, what's your son going to do, for heaven's sake? You better worry about yourself before you worry about somebody else. Gina's not a little kid anymore. Look at yourself. Look in the mirror. Listen, of course I know you're her mother. I know you love her very much, but you know what? All she cares about is when she can take her next drug. You have to remember that. You can't afford to get sick. Your son needs you. You have to stay healthy. Let God take care of Gina. You need to take care of yourself and your son."

My sister was right, I thought.

My son needed me more than anybody.

After that I just stayed away from Gina.

But every time I went to my sister's, I passed by Ruben's house and I would try to see Gina and see what she was doing.

I would just drive by, though, and I would say to myself, "Let her do what she wants to do," while I tried to peek in through Ruben's windows.

I stopped praying.

One day I got a call about Gina from a doctor in the emergency room of a hospital. He was leaving a message that Gina was in a car accident and was in very serious condition. I picked up the phone while he was still talking.

"How bad is she?" I asked him.

"Pretty bad. I think you should come down here," he said.

"What hospital?"

"Bridgeport."

When the doctor called, my son was right next to me. He heard everything.

"Who's that?" he asked.

"Who do you think? It's your sister," I said. "She's in the emergency room of the hospital."

"Are you going to see her?" he asked.

"Yes, I will, but not right now."

"Why not?"

"I don't feel well today. I've got a terrible headache and a stomachache, too. I'm just going to go lay down and go to bed. Maybe when I get up, I'll think about it. Now I just feel dizzy."

I went in and lay down on my bed and I didn't even get up the next day. I kept telling my son, when he came in, not to wake me up. I needed my sleep.

Two days later I got up early in the morning, put my clothes on and I went to see Gina.

When I went into her hospital room, I looked at her in the bed and couldn't see her face. Her head was wrapped completely in bandages. I could only see her eyes. Her hand was in a cast and so was her leg.

I sat down. She was in such pain she couldn't talk. When I said something to her, she could just wink her eye in response.

Tears came to her eyes as I talked to her.

I sat there silently for a while until I couldn't stand being next to her any longer because she was in such pain. I went to the nurse's desk and asked the doctor if Gina was going to be all right.

"About fifty-fifty," he said. "There are a few bones broken in her leg. And her knee. And her arm. She's hurting pretty bad."

"You know, doctor," I said, "This isn't the first time she's been here, but this time is the worst."

Because she was in intensive care, no one was allowed to see her except me. I went back in and sat next to her.

She couldn't drink water through her mouth herself. The nurse had to help her sip with a long straw.

Her mouth was always so dry so I took a little cotton swab and dipped it in her water then swabbed it gently all around her lips. She opened her mouth a little bit and put her tongue on the damp swab.

I finally left and as I drove home, I cried like a baby.

I felt so guilty and I couldn't tell anyone what happened to her. Not even my sister or my mother. All I said to my son was that she had gotten a little scratched up and that she was going into detox. She wasn't coming home.

I couldn't tell him the truth.

I didn't call anybody. I just kept to myself. I felt so bad that I hadn't helped her, but she never listened.

After my sister had told me not to help Gina out anymore, I felt I had to talk to someone so I saw a psychiatrist, just to have a person to talk to. He told me I didn't have to do anything for her anymore.

No one knew what I had gone through except me, myself. Even after I had talked to the psychiatrist, I still felt bad. His talk had been cheap, I guess.

I finally stopped talking to everyone.

I went and visited Gina almost every day. I took my son with me if I had to. She was in the hospital almost six months.

Gina must have nine lives, I sometimes thought, and I wondered how—and why—God was keeping her alive.

Sometimes she would be talking and I couldn't understand at all what she was talking about. The drugs and alcohol had begun to take over her mind.

One day my mother asked me where Gina was. She hadn't heard from her for a long time. She wanted to know if she was all right.

My mother missed Gina very much. Gina had been taking care of her for a while and then one day, she just stopped. She had been giving her money, but after that accident she didn't talk to her again.

I finally went to see my mom and explained what had happened. She had started asking about Gina every day.

When she heard, she started crying.

"I knew it," she said. "I knew something must have happened to her. For all these years, even when she was sick and could barely pick up the phone, Gina would call me to see how I was doing. She was the only one who always talked to me and who always cared for me. I know you're my daughter, but she was more supportive than you. Gina has always been nice to me."

My mother asked me to please take her to see Gina in the hospital.

"Are you sure, mom?" I asked.

"I'm sure. She'll love to hear my voice. I would always tell her, when something happened to her, 'Be strong.' She needs me. She needs my voice. Please take me to see her."

I told my mom I would pick her up the next morning.

When we got there the next day, my mom held Gina's hand and she kissed her face. She told Gina she had been worried about her and had known something bad had happened to her because she had not called her.

She saw that both of Gina's hands were in casts and I think she realized Gina couldn't have called her.

I left the two of them to talk by themselves for a while, and when I came back, I could see that Gina was more alert.

The doctor came in and after talking to Gina, he pulled me aside and had told me that he thought she was becoming herself again. She was talking a little bit. He thought everything was going to be okay and that Gina would get her head bandages off in a few more weeks.

I had been afraid she was not going to make it.

She was still in a lot of pain, though, and they were giving her a lot of drugs, both morphine and other pain pills.

After we left, my mom asked me why I had hidden the accident from her. I told her I hadn't wanted her to be hurt.

"You don't know what love is," she told me. "Gina and I are so different from you. I understand her. You and your sister don't understand her. But I do. How could you neglect your own flesh and blood? That is not God's way. No matter what, you have to stick with her. And unless you tell me what's going on, I won't know. From now on you cannot neglect her. She's young. She went out into the world too soon. She thinks she's doing the right thing, but she does the wrong thing. God still loves her, but she never really learned enough self discipline from you or your husband. Shame on you."

I told my mother I knew that, but it was too late.

She told me nothing was too late. I could always start all over.

As Gina recovered, I spent less time with her. I had things I had to do for my son which I'd neglected and I still had a part time job, too.

One day I picked up my mom again to go see Gina and I brought my son too.

Gina was happy that day and she laughed for the first time since I'd been going to the hospital. She hadn't seen her brother for a long while. She had always sent cards to her brother when she wasn't around or mailed him a little note from time to time. She cared about him.

That day she seemed more alert than I'd see her for a long time.

As we left, I asked Gina if she needed anything. She said she wanted something to put on her lips because they were still so very dry.

The next time I came, I brought her Chapstick and a whole grocery bag full of different little containers of juice she could drink.

Gina still couldn't walk because her knee had been broken, but after the visits with her grandmother and brother, she herself was feeling better.

One day she told me that she knew she had told me time after time that she wanted to do something different with her life and that she had fallen apart over and over again. This time, though, was different, she said. She had just been mixed up. She didn't know how she was going to repay me and make up for all the damage she'd done to me and to her grandma and her brother.

And to herself, she said.

Suddenly she started crying uncontrollably.

Finally she told me she thought God was punishing her because she had said she was going to straighten herself out so many times, but she never did. She had hurt too many people because of that. Now God was hurting her, she said, because God wanted her to feel how she had hurt others.

I told her I understood. I had done the same thing myself.

Chapter One

When I was about twelve years old, my aunt took care of me.

When my aunt wasn't home, I'd take her cigarettes and smoke them. Sometimes she let me go out with the other neighborhood kids.

My mom never knew what I was doing at my aunt's.

When I went out with the neighbors' kids, we would hang around at the local gas stations and smoke cigarettes. Nobody warned me about smoking and about what cigarettes would do. When you're little, you like to do the things that adults do. You think it's fun.

After a while I met some boys who smoked grass. At first I thought it was like a regular cigarette. We were all young and all we thought about was having fun.

My mom thought I was babysitting or at home with my aunt.

When I turned thirteen, I looked like I was sixteen. I had grown old fast and I looked older than all my friends.

I didn't have much education. I went to high school, but I didn't pay much attention. All I did was hang around and take drugs and drink.

I had started to drink beer when I was twelve. I tried hard liquor too. I was so young, I'd drink and just go to sleep. As the days went by, I became addicted to liquor. I started to drink all the time, whatever I was doing.

Once, after I'd been drinking, I was walking across an old footbridge, but I didn't notice the bridge was broken. I fell off it and fell down into a gully almost thirty feet below. I hurt myself, but that was only the first of many accidents.

I spent time with my aunt or with my grandma, but I really had no one to tell me that I shouldn't be drinking and doing drugs. I guess I knew that they were bad, but I figured that God couldn't make the good in the world without making the bad, too, or otherwise we'd never know the difference. I figured God understood.

He must have understood me, too, even if I didn't.

I'd usually take some liquor and meet the other boys and girls down on Main Street in Bridgeport. Before I went home, I'd gargle with Listerine and chew a lot of gum so no one could smell the alcohol. When I got home, I'd just go directly to bed and fall asleep.

I used to go to sleep by myself then, but I always remembered that when I was little, my father would come in to my bedroom every night and read me a story or sing me to sleep.

When I lived with my aunt, I had no one to tuck me into bed so I went outside her home to find affection and love. I had friends in the street, and the alcohol and the drugs warmed me up just as if I was being held by someone who loved me.

I believed my dad still loved me, even if I never saw him, and I thought maybe God loved me, too, even though I never saw him either.

But the drugs and the booze I could always see and feel.

One night we got caught by the police.

We had drunk so much liquor and had smoked so much grass that we all fell asleep on the sidewalk. When I opened my eyes, I was in the police station. I was in such a stupor that when the police carried me to the station, I thought it was my father carrying me upstairs to my bed.

The policeman called my mother. I was almost fourteen then, but my mother got so angry that I wasn't allowed to go out at all after that. I couldn't even go to my aunt's or to my grandma's.

I was home by myself the next day and I knew where my father kept his liquor. I went and got it and drank it. Then I ran away.

I stayed on the streets for a while and then finally I moved in with my grandma back in Bridgeport.

My mother and I didn't get along after that. Every time she tried to do something for me, I would turn away from her. I wouldn't even talk to her.

I was still drinking. I couldn't stop.

I'd sneak out and meet my old friends on the streets of Bridgeport. One night we were hanging around at one gas station and policeman caught us smoking a joint. He took us to the police station.

I called my mom.

She asked me where I was and when I told her, she said she'd come pick me up.

On the way home in the car I was tired and I was freezing because I didn't have enough clothes on. It was winter.

I told my mom I was sorry. I was so mixed up, I didn't know what to say to her. I started crying. I told her I knew I was hurting her, but that when I was younger, I had so much love from her and from dad. Then things changed.

She started to cry. She told me she just had too many things she had to do. My brother took all her time. My father was divorcing her. She said she didn't have anybody to turn to either.

Even she didn't know what to do.

She said she had gotten married very young, when she was seventeen, and now she was paying for that mistake. She'd be paying for it for a long time, she told me. God was punishing her.

I didn't know what to say to her. I felt like I was part of the mistake, part of her punishment.

I kept hanging around with my old friends. One night we were just sitting around in the train station smoking grass and drinking a lot. I don't know exactly what happened, but there was one boy there who was older than I and he somehow stumbled outside and down onto the tracks. A train was passing quickly through the station, didn't see him in time and ran him over. He died immediately.

I started drinking even more then.

My mother finally put me in detox, but I wasn't there a month.

I was sick because I still needed liquor and I still needed drugs. So I left.

My dad came and picked me up from my grandma's one day and drove me to New York to see a psychiatrist. He said afterward it was the doctor's fault that I hadn't stopped drinking and doing drugs.

When I went to the psychiatrist, he just talked and I didn't listen. All that was on my mind when I sat there was how was I going to get some drugs when I got home that day. That's all. I have no idea what that psychiatrist said.

My dad took me to other psychiatrists, too, and he kept saying it was their fault that I didn't feel better.

He really didn't understand anything because he was drunk himself.

Before he and my mom separated, he'd just come home, eat his dinner and go upstairs and pass out. He'd start drinking again the next morning. Before it was even twelve o'clock, he would already have had several drinks. All he drank was vodka. He seldom ate.

On the weekend mornings he'd start to drink as soon as he got up. He'd go outside and sit on the porch with his bottle.

Sometimes my mom would join him and they'd drink all day. I'd leave and go out with my friends. My mom would give me money if I told her I needed clothes. I'd take her money and go and buy drugs. She was too drunk to know.

I got deeper and deeper into that life and no one could handle me. There was no one home to handle me.

I was wild.

After my third time in jail, my mom threw me out again and I started living with my friends.

One friend, Jamie, who was older than I, brought me to his home, a big, beautiful house with more than twenty rooms. There was a beautiful swimming pool in the middle of a huge yard isolated by tall wooden fences from the neighbors. It took a while to drive all the way down the long driveway and you couldn't see the neighbors' houses at all along the way. The house was a mansion.

Suddenly I felt I'd seen what real life was for the first time.

He'd sneak me in and put me in one of the many empty rooms. I'd fall asleep immediately. The next morning I'd get up very early and wait for him to take me back to the street. Sometimes, when his parents were having a party, he'd bring me home and feed me dinner there.

I met his parents a few times. They were different than mine because they were so strict. My friend was eighteen and even though I was only fourteen, I looked much older, especially because I was so tall. I had wrinkles in my face, too, from so much drinking and drugs.

One day his mother asked me if I wasn't too old to hang around with her son. I should hang around with people my own age, she said.

She could tell I was not the same kind of girl as her son's other female friends. Every time I went there, she gave me a dirty look. I would just sit beside her son and say nothing. I didn't drink when she was around, just soda.

One night there was a huge party at their house with both adults and kids. As the sun went down I was very stoned and sitting outside in the yard by myself, watching the beautiful sunset.

His mother came up to me and said she didn't want to see me around there anymore. I was a bad influence on her son.

I didn't say anything.

I knew her son better than she did. He was the one who got drugs for us. His mother still didn't even know that he was drinking and taking drugs.

She said to me, "Gina, you're a pretty girl, but you make me depressed. I've read about your parents in the newspaper a few times when they got arrested for domestic disturbances. You're nothing but a tramp and a whore. I really don't want to see you around anymore. I'm sorry. Your mother's a beautiful woman, too—I've seen her around town—but I want you to stay away from my son."

I felt bad when she called me a tramp and a whore. I'd never thought of myself that way. No one had ever called me that before and it bothered me for a long time.

I couldn't tell her son about it, but I asked Jamie to take me to my grandma's.

I never went back to his house again. Jamie would invite me, but I wouldn't go.

A few days later I called my mom and told her I needed money.

"Listen, sweetheart," she said. I could tell she was drunk. "Call your dad." She hung up the phone.

After I set the phone down, I started crying.

I called my father then. He had moved out from my mom and brother by then.

"I wish you'd never called me," he said. "I'm not going to give you money. You know what you'll do with it. You'll just buy more drugs. I will never give you any more money. I will never give you anything. If you want something, get a job. I am washing my hands of you. I'm finished."

He hung up.

I got in more and more trouble after that.

I was in jail a lot, but my mother would never answer the phone when I called her. She wouldn't write back to me when I wrote her a letter either.

I didn't talk to her or hear from her for about two years.

I finally ended up in the hospital after another motorcycle accident, but Ruben came by and said he was going to drive me to Florida.

We'd have fun, he promised.

Ruben picked me right up out of my bed in the hospital and carried me into the hallway. He set me down in a wheel chair that was parked against the wall and then wheeled me out into the parking lot to a shiny new black Cadillac sedan.

In a few minutes we were driving south on I-95 and headed for Miami.

We stopped when we got to New Jersey because all I had on was my hospital robe. I lay in the car so nobody could see me and Ruben ran into a Sears and picked me up a pair of shorts and a tee shirt.

We drove through the night and the next morning stopped at a beach in North Carolina.

Ruben was half American and half Spanish. His mother came from Puerto Rico, but his father had been born in Miami and Ruben still had many relatives there.

We slept for a little while in the sand, lying together on my hospital robe, and then woke up and watched the waves for a while.

I asked Ruben about his father because no one in his home had ever mentioned him and I was curious.

He said his father and mother hadn't gotten along. When Ruben was little—five or six—his father drank a lot. He always yelled at his kids and hit them. One time he hit Ruben hard in his eye and his eye became bloodshot and swelled up badly. When he went to school the next day, his teacher asked him what happened to him. He didn't want to get his father into trouble so he told the teacher he had fallen.

His father hit him many times. One time he twisted his arm and almost broke it before his mother stopped him. Every time his mother tried to defend Ruben, his father hit her. Once he picked Ruben's mother up in the air and then threw her down to the floor. She couldn't get up. He had broken her back.

Ruben said because he and his brothers were so little, they couldn't help her. They could only watch.

The only one he wouldn't touch was Ruben's sister, Juanita, maybe because she was a girl. He always hit the boys, though, over and over again. Ruben told me his father almost killed his brother once. He couldn't remember what is brother had done, something about the TV, but he threw his brother across the living room and he had hit his head against the far wall. He couldn't get up. Ruben's mother went crazy. She screamed and screamed, but his brother was unconscious and she finally got the car and took him to the hospital.

Ruben said his father was a good provider, though. They always had food, always had a home. The only thing wrong with him was that he had a very bad temper.

One night Ruben and his family were watching TV. Ruben was enjoying the movie so much he had forgotten all that was bothering him. He was seven then. His father came in and started screaming and chased everyone upstairs. Even though all the boys were interested in the movie, they didn't dare watch the end. They just ran upstairs, the three boys. Downstairs Ruben's father kept screaming at his mother.

Ruben tiptoed partially down the stairs and saw his dad punching her again and again as if she were a punching bag.

He would never forget that.

Ruben went back to the boys' room and closed the door so his two brothers couldn't hear. He turned their radio up very loud.

The next day Ruben was watching a movie on TV and saw a man hold a gun up to someone and shot him. Ruben got the idea to kill his father. That way he could protect his brothers and mother from his father.

Ruben started practicing how he wanted to kill him.

One night his father came home while they were all watching TV. His father started screaming at them and Ruben went out to the garbage bag in the kitchen. His father thought Ruben was going to take the garbage out so he wouldn't get yelled at for not having done it earlier.

Instead Ruben picked out the gun he had hidden there.

"I think this is enough," he said to his father. "You've given us a lot of headaches. You're never satisfied with what our mom does around here, yet she works like a dog. I've had it with you. This is enough. After today we won't have to worry about you anymore."

Ruben fired the gun twice, once into his heart and once into his head.

His father fell and lay still on the floor.

"Mom," Ruben said, "You don't have to worry about things any more. Nobody's going to hit you anymore. We're going to live in peace from now on."

His mother screamed and then called the police.

The police took him, but he was only seven so they put him in a detention center for children who had gotten in trouble. He was only there for a while because he was so young.

When he got out, he told his mom that he was sorry, but that he had to do it. He had no other way.

His mom hugged him and said she loved him.

After Ruben finished his story, we both were silent for some time.

Finally I took his hand and I went back to the car and lay down across the back seat. Ruben lay beside me. We started to make love.

Suddenly the door was ripped open and two policemen were holding guns on us.

"You stole this car," shouted one policeman to Ruben.

We were taken to the police station and they put Ruben in jail. I was told I could go back home.

I called my mother to send me money so I could come home, but she hung up on me.

I started to worry and went back to the police station desk and told them they had to keep me there.

The policeman said I had to go home.

"Call your parents and have them send you money," he told me.

I called my mom over and over again, but she would not come to the phone. I had given her too many headaches. She didn't want to know me. She didn't want to hear from me.

I kept calling and calling her.

"I want to come home, mom," I would say into her answering machine. "Please, mom," I would beg her and tell her I knew I caused her a lot of trouble.

She wouldn't pick up the phone.

I found out later my brother had heard my messages and finally begged her to send me money so I could at least come back up to Connecticut.

I left her the number at the police station where she could call me.

Two hours later I was still at the police station and getting hungry and getting thirsty. I didn't have any money. All I could do was drink a little water.

Finally a policeman came over to me and said my mother was on the phone.

I explained to her what had happened and she said she would get me a plane ticket to get me home, but that was all.

When I got home, I told her I was serious that I wanted to get help, but she wouldn't help me.

I called a place myself and my aunt helped me get in. I went to Yale New Haven Hospital and their special drug rehabilitation program. My aunt took me there and I stayed for two months.

While I was there, I took everything seriously and I was given methadone to ease me through my withdrawal.

I wrote my mom a letter and told her that I knew I had put her through a lot and asked her to understand what drugs and alcohol do to a person. I told her I didn't think she understood because, when people are using drugs, they're not themselves. They're evil. I told her I hoped she prayed to God every day and night that I would do the right thing when I got out of rehab and that God would help me to be strong and guide me in the right direction.

I told her I wanted to make her proud of me. I knew I hadn't been what she had wanted me to be, but I told her I was finally changed. I said I was even thinking of settling down, getting married and having my own family.

One night while I was there I got down on my knees and prayed to God to give me courage and strength to be what I could be. I knew I could get better.

I worked hard day in and day out and felt I was getting better each day. The days started going by faster and faster.

I wrote my mother again that, no matter what, I hoped everything was okay with her. I told her I was okay there and that no matter how hard it was for me to go through, I knew that I could be strong. I thought God was on my side. I needed his help. I knew I would get better, I told her, and that when I got home I wanted to get a job and work like a normal person.

I promised her that I would do better and told her that I loved her and that I would write her again the next week.

I kept writing her, but she never wrote me back.

Chapter Two

My father and mother had separated by then and my father began a new life. He had moved to Florida and he then got married again after divorcing my mom.

I had nowhere to go when I got out of Yale New Haven. I didn't want to go to my grandma's. I had always gone to her and cried on her shoulder.

My grandma would always talk to me. No matter what. She was the best. But I didn't want to be a burden to her anymore.

I went to live with my father in Florida for a while. He was talking to me again.

I had met a boy, Joe, who came to visit me one day at my dad's and we smoked a joint together in my room. My father had come home for lunch unexpectedly and came into my room and saw what we were doing. He was furious. He started to hit Joe, but it was not the boy's fault. I had gotten the grass, not him.

But I didn't tell my father that.

My father picked Joe up by his armpits and threw him out of the house onto the front lawn.

My father was so mad, he couldn't see straight. He stormed back inside, then went back outside and I thought he was going to go back to work, but he came right back in again. I thought he had forgotten something because he was so mad.

Instead he just walked around the house once, went back out and drove off to work.

Later that morning the phone rang. A doctor from the hospital told me my father had been electrocuted. He was dead.

He was supposed to turn off the main electricity before he worked on one machine at work, but he must have forgotten. He started to cut a wire and he was electrocuted.

He died because of me.

I couldn't take enough drugs to ease my pain.

I called my grandma and told her I was coming home. She asked if I was okay and I told her I was fine. I just asked her not to call my mom.

I lived with her for a little while and I started hanging around the same motor-cycle guys I had hung around with before in Bridgeport. I was taking all kinds of drugs. I was really down and I couldn't quit.

I didn't want to.

One day I was hanging around the street and we were doing cocaine and heroin, speedballs, shooting them up in Beardsley Park. Suddenly three police cars drove up. I threw down my drugs and ran away, but some of the others got caught.

The next day my mother called my grandma and told her the police had come by looking for me. They wanted to put me in jail, they said, because my friends had had turned me in.

I took the phone and said hello to her for the first time in a couple years.

"Now they're looking for you too," she said.

I didn't want to go back to jail.

My father's parents lived in Nova Scotia in those days, and my mother called them to see if they could come down and bring me back to live them for a while. She didn't really tell them why, just that I needed a "vacation."

I packed a suitcase, including the heroin I still had, hidden in baby powder, so I wouldn't be caught by customs. The next day we took off for Canada with my grandma and grandpa. Because they were so old, the customs officials didn't search us very thoroughly and they found none of the drugs I had with me.

I stayed in Nova Scotia for a while with my grandparents. It was a beautiful quiet place and I liked it there.

One afternoon my cousin went for a motorcycle ride with her boyfriend and they had a terrible accident. Both were killed.

I had had two bad motorcycle accidents myself by then. Once I broke my knee and scraped all the skin off my leg. I was in the hospital a long time healing. The second motorcycle accident was after my boyfriend had snorted too much cocaine. He thought he was fine, but we had an accident and again I was in the hospital for a long time. My neck was broken. My ribs and one arm were broken. I ended up with permanent scars.

These two kids, my cousin and her boyfriend were both good kids.

It suddenly seemed to me that I should have been the one who'd been killed. I was a wild person. I drove people crazy. Yet this couple went out one sunny after-noon for a motorcycle ride, and they were the ones who got killed.

It wasn't fair.

I kept asking myself why I was the one who was still alive. They didn't do drugs. They didn't drink. They were just nice kids.

I was not a nice kid.

I didn't understand. I had all these accidents. I was in and out of rehab. I could no longer count how many times I'd been in and out of jail.

Yet I managed to survive.

Why would God do that?

Life was different in Nova Scotia. My grandparents there had lived there all their lives. They had a little farm and they raised vegetables. They had animals, too. The people in their community did a lot of fishing, mostly for lobsters and crab.

These people had no problems. These people were kind. They were patient. They weren't metropolitan in any way. The girls all had long hair and they didn't even wear any make up.

It was God's country.

I stayed there for five months, but it became too much for me. I was haunted by the death of my cousin and her boyfriend. I wanted to go back to Bridgeport. I started crying a lot and I started calling my mom and telling her that I should have died because I had ruined myself. I didn't deserve to be alive.

Finally I went back to Bridgeport.

I lived with my grandma. I was supposed to get an apartment, but I couldn't afford one because I was spending all my money again on drugs.

I hung around with my old friends, and we were all alike. We took every drug we could get our hands on.

I was so addicted to drugs, I couldn't get away from them. I couldn't quit. My mother finally convinced me to go into rehab again. I went into several different rehab programs, but I ran away from each of them.

Finally I went to a rehab facility in Newtown. I stayed there for almost two years, but I was taking drugs all the time I was there. One visitor after another would come and bring us all drugs. None of us ever quit.

After twenty months there, I came home. I was supposed to get a job, but I couldn't work. I could no longer concentrate. All I did was take more drugs.

Even though I had no money, I would find different ways to get them. Usually I would just go out with a guy who did drugs or sold them so he would give them to me to sell and to take.

I started living with a guy I'd met in rehab. He was able to get one powerful drug, Cannabinol. It was a mixture of several hard drugs, but you could only take a little bit of it. You sniffed it like cocaine.

When I took it, I no longer recognized anyone around me. I didn't know what I was doing.

I lived with him and we made our money selling the drug. One day the police raided our apartment while we were both there because he had sold the Cannabinol to a young boy, but it was too strong for him and after he took it, he ended up killing another boy. He had gone to jail and he turned us in.

We both went to jail for just over four months.

I kept falling back into drugs over and over again. The same pattern.

I was stopped by a policeman while I was driving my grandma's car one day and he found cocaine in the glove compartment.

I went to jail for another four months.

When I got out, I had no job, no money, no nothing. Zero.

It was November and it was cold. I didn't have a lot of clothes, just what I'd been wearing when they picked me up four months earlier, when it was still warm weather. I walked the street until I found a phone and called some friends, but I couldn't reach anyone.

I didn't want to bother a man I had come to call my guardian angel because I hadn't called him for a long time. He had been my manager many years ago at Friendly's and he had helped me out several times with money or a place to crash overnight. He liked me, I guessed. Maybe I was like his daughter. He never asked me any questions.

I walked along Main Street, Bridgeport, until it got dark. It was freezing by then and I was miserable. I decided to call my mom again anyway and I left a message telling her I was freezing and I'd just gotten out of jail again for drugs. I called my aunt, but there was no answer there either. I didn't want to call my grandma because she was sick. She couldn't drive either.

I kept walking just to keep warm and suddenly a car pulled up beside me. I walked over to the car and tried to look inside, but I couldn't see the driver. I figured maybe I could turn an easy trick. Suddenly a man leaned across the seat and swung open the passenger door and grabbed me by my shirt. He pulled me in and closed the door.

He was a huge black man.

I just wanted to get out of there. He pulled at my pants and tore them off me. I tried to scream, but he hit me on the head very hard and I lost consciousness. While I was out, he started raping me.

I came to, but didn't want to fight him off because I was afraid he would kill me. He finished raping me and I lost consciousness again for a moment. He pushed me out of the car with his foot and down onto the sidewalk.

He hit me again and even though I had come to, I pretended I was still out. He pushed me on my back, he kicked my stomach with his right foot, and I just pretended I was dead.

I started to wish I were dead because his beating me hurt so badly.

Finally he got back in his car and drove off.

I lay on the pavement for a while and then struggled up. I was freezing.

I realized I was not too far from my guardian angel's house. I didn't know what else to do but go there.

I walked there and knocked on his door. He was home.

By the time he had opened the door, I could no longer feel my feet or my hands. They were numb.

I stepped into his front hall and my body collapsed. I couldn't push it any further.

He was in shock. He dragged me into his bathroom and ran warm water into the tub. He knew that hot water would have been too great a shock to my body. He took all my clothes off, picked me up and told me everything would be okay.

He wanted to soak me in the tub, but I had blood all over my face and forehead and I could tell he wasn't completely sure what to do.

H decided to put me in the tub. He washed my body off, lifted me out, dried me and then blew dry my hair. I was completely limp still.

He went into the bedroom and spread an electric blanket across the bed and came back to me and said, "Get on the bed. I didn't call the ambulance, Gina, because I was afraid by the time they got here, you might not have made it."

He was a smart man.

"You saved my life," I said.

He tucked me into the bed and the electric blanket continued to warm up my body after the hot bath. He went into the kitchen and warmed up some soup for me. He brought the bowl in and tried to feed me himself, but I could only swallow a couple of spoonfuls.

I just wanted to close my eyes so I could forget everything that had happened.

I told him that my body was in pain and that I hadn't been able to feel the bruises before because I was so cold. He gave me some aspirin.

"Did somebody hit you?" he asked.

"No. I fell after my feet slid on the snow and I hit my head on a rock.

The next morning my head had bumps and there were thick, dark scabs on my cuts. He took me to a doctor and I told the doctor I fell. He kept asking me what had happened to me. He wanted to hear more than what I had told him, more than that I had slipped on the snow and banged my head on a rock.

He told me I was lucky I hadn't been killed.

I didn't want to say anything that would be reported to the police at that time because the police knew I had started to work as a prostitute again. I didn't want the police hassling me. I needed the money.

"You could get killed," my guardian angel told me on the way home. I think he knew I hadn't fallen in the snow. "You almost died. Your hands are black and blue. So are your legs. And your face. Why didn't you call your mom?"

"I did call my mom, many times. She never answered the phone."

"She never calls you back?"

"No. I wrote her a lot of letters too, but she's never answered. I had no place to go finally, so I came here."

"You can stay with me as long as you want."

Chapter Three

My guardian angel told me, "You look so old." I was only eighteen then. I decided I didn't want to do drugs any more.

I stayed with him and hoped I had learned my lesson, but I started to feel sorry for him. He really cared for me, and I didn't want to hurt him like I had hurt everyone else. I woke up one day and decided I had to put myself back in rehab again to protect him.

I went into rehab at Fairfield Hills and I stayed dry for two months. No liquor. No drugs.

The days continued to go by and suddenly I noticed I was not so unhappy. I felt stronger. I exercised. I walked.

One morning I got out of bed and went into my bathroom. When I looked in the mirror, I noticed that my face was still broken out and that I still had dark circles under my eyes that made me look like I was thirty-five years old even though I was not even twenty.

I had so many pimples on my face that I looked like I had hives

I went to the kitchen and got a paper cup and filled it with Clorox. I went back to the bathroom and dabbed my face all over with the Clorox because I knew it killed bacteria.

Every day after that I put a little Clorox on my face, and eventually the pimples went away.

My skin was rough and dry when I touched it. I asked my aunt to bring me some moisturizer the next time she visited me. I told her I also needed scissors. I was going to trim my hair myself.

She brought me a moisturizer, a good cleanser and some other creams to cure my face. They worked. I looked better and better as the days went by.

I was beginning to take care of myself.

I hadn't even looked in a mirror for a long time. All I did was drink, do drugs and sleep

My aunt had brought me scissors, too. My hair was dyed black and was long, but very bushy, very curly. I had no blow drier, nothing to take care of it. I had just been washing it and letting it dry itself.

I took the scissors and cut off almost all my hair off. It was so short that it looked like bristles, but my face looked good and everybody said they liked it. They thought I'd gone out to a beauty salon.

I looked nice for the first time in a very long time.

I felt good, mentally and physically. I was happy, too. I wanted to stay straightened out.

I told my aunt I thought they were going to let me go home soon. If I continued to do well, they might even let me go early.

I tried hard to improve myself so I could go back home to grandma's.

One night, before I left, we had a party. We had dancing and had a special dinner. The next day I wrote my mom again. I had taken some pictures so she could see what I looked like. She hadn't seen me for a very long time.

I told my mom I thought I had really improved myself and that I was happier. When I came here, I used to weigh a hundred pounds. Now I weighed one hundred and fifteen. I looked good, I told her, and I felt good and hoped I would go home soon.

I told her that before I went to bed I always prayed and that I prayed for her and for grandma. I asked her to tell grandma I would see her soon and that I loved her, but that I loved her, my mom, the most, and that she was always in my heart.

She finally wrote back to me and invited me home.

After another three months, they let me go.

I felt different and I went home and I lived with my mother.

The first few weeks I didn't really do anything except go for long walks. Finally I got used to the world again.

One day I took a train into New York just to walk around. My mom had given me a little money and said I should take myself to New York as a reward.

I put on one of my mom's suits and I took the train in. When I got there, I walked up and down Madison Avenue looking in all the store windows.

I found a restaurant and read the prices on the menu in the window and decided to go in to eat. Inside the customers all looked like executives and business people. The women all wore suits.

I looked nice, too, and I went into the ladies room and put on a little make up. I had finally realized I was attractive. My mom was attractive too. She was even prettier than I when she was young, but I looked a lot like her. I was well built and when I wore her suit, I felt I looked like a woman with class.

I ordered a soft drink at the bar and stood there for a while when a gentleman came over to talk to me. He said he thought I worked around there.

After a while I went out and walked around some more and then found another place to go into, another nice restaurant. There was a piano bar and I just stood there and looked around. The other women there looked rich and I knew they were well educated, too. I also knew I was not.

Finally I left and went home early. I didn't want to stay too late and when I got home, I told my mom that I'd been to those two places.

I began thinking that maybe I should get a job in New York City. I could commute, but if I had to work nights, I wasn't sure how I could come home.

I told my mom I thought I would like to get a job in New York if I could get a job that would pay me enough money to do things for myself. I wanted to get a nice pocketbook and all the other things a girl needs. I wanted to go to beauty salons and do all the things I had never done before.

My mom gave me some money to go to a beauty salon and get my hair done professionally. That was the first time in my life that I had been pampered. It was nice.

I told my mom that I wanted to do that for myself, but I had to get a job first.

A week later I went back to New York. I went back to the restaurant where all the executives had been and I sat down by myself and ordered something to eat. I sat in the bar, but I didn't drink.

The gentleman who had spoken to me before came into the bar and started talking to me again. I stayed there just to listen to him, but I didn't say much myself because I was frightened of saying something wrong. I had never talked to a man like this in my whole life. I just listened to him. He asked me if I would be back there again and I told him I wasn't from there, I was from Bridgeport, Connecticut. He told me he hoped he would see me soon.

I told him, "Me, too," and I left.

I went home and told my mom all about my trip.

She told me that I was a beautiful girl and in the city, I had to be very careful who I talked to. It was better not to go out with anybody except the people I knew.

So I was careful.

I went back again to the restaurant again. I didn't put a lot of make up on, just a little lipstick and a little mascara. I saw the same man and he told me his name was Christopher. He was nice. He was polite. I thought he must have a good job.

He told me we should get together, but I told him my mom said I shouldn't go out with strangers so I would only meet him there at the restaurant.

He gave me his card.

Eventually I told him I had to go home, but said maybe the next time we could go out. I felt like I knew him now.

A few weeks later I went back there again.

Christopher was there. He had been coming every day, he said, waiting for me to return. I sat down to talk with him and he asked to take me out to dinner. I refused because I had decided I didn't want him to move that fast with me. I said maybe next time.

He asked if he could call me and I gave him my mom's home phone and my grandma's. I told him he had to talk loudly when he talked to my grandma because she was old and couldn't hear well.

I went back to that restaurant four times altogether to meet Christopher and then, on the fifth time we met, I accepted a date with him.

We went out for steak at a restaurant that was fancy. Everyone was wearing a suit. The waitress was pretty and nice, and I was a little embarrassed. My clothes didn't fit in there. My mom's dress looked good, but I knew I needed richer clothes in order to fit in with Christopher at a place like that.

I told Christopher I wasn't comfortable going to such a nice place where everyone was in such beautiful clothes.

"Are you kidding?," he said. "You look beautiful. "I never met a girl as pretty as you in all my life."

He made me feel really good.

I was relaxed with him. He was calm. He talked slowly. I started to enjoy the way he presented himself to me. I hadn't met a man like that. The men I knew were young and immature. They didn't know how to treat a girl. This man did. I felt I understood him and he understood me.

He had a good job, I think, but I hadn't asked him what he did because I didn't want him to ask me what I did.

He told me not to eat too much dinner because they had such delicious desserts. I told him that once before I had continued stuffing myself and I had dessert too, and when I went home, I didn't feel too well. That food had been good, but heavy. I wasn't going to do that again tonight.

He told me he thought I enjoyed sweets and that I should have dessert. I joked with him that I didn't need anything sweet because he was already sweet.

He started laughing and told me I was pretty funny.

He asked if he should order a bottle of wine and I said no because I had to go home and I didn't want to fall asleep on the train. I told him I didn't care for wine and he said he only drank on special occasions. Otherwise he didn't drink at all.

I asked if he was born in New York and he said no, he came from Europe. I was comfortable asking him questions now and I began to feel like we were having a real conversation finally.

He asked me if I came from a big family and I told him my mom had two boys and me, just three altogether.

"That's not many," he said.

"How about you?" I asked.

"My own parents died when I was little. I have foster parents, but they act like my parents. They've taken care of me since I was little. I adore them. I go visit them in Europe on holidays or when I'm on trips or vacations."

"You didn't have any brothers or sisters?"

"Not that I know of," he said.

He asked if I knew much about New York and I told him I didn't and had only just started coming here. I told him my parents had brought me here once in a while when I was a little girl and that now I liked the city. It was so different from where I came from.

He thanked me for joining him for dinner and told me how much he was enjoying my company.

Instead of dessert, I had coffee.

Mostly I didn't talk a lot, though, that night. I was interested in him and I just listened to what he said.

After dinner we went outside and started walking. It was a pretty night. There was a fresh breeze and we walked and walked.

Finally I told him I hated to leave him, but I had to get on the train. He flagged a taxi and took me to the train station.

He told me he wanted to see me again and that he hoped I'd move to New York so we could go to movies and shows together. He loved to go to shows because they made him relax.

As I got onto my train, I thanked him and told him how much I had enjoyed our dinner. He gave me a kiss and hugged me.

He was sweet.

On the train I began thinking how lucky I was to meet this man.

I was happy. I needed a friend.

All I had was God.

I had been thinking. I didn't know if I wanted to move to New York, get a job there and have an apartment. It was tiring taking the train back and forth, but I wondered if maybe I wasn't used to it. A lot of people did it.

New York was so different. The people were nice, but busy. They dressed well. Many women wore gloves and their hair was always done. Everything matched.

I told my mom that one day when I had enough money I was going to buy an outfit to go out in and that everything would match, my shoes, my purse, my clothes.

I knew I was thinking big.

My mom said that would be good for me.

Suddenly she said to me, "You know, Gina, I got married when I was eighteen and I had a kid at the same time. Don't you do that. I knew it was not good to marry that young. But that's what happened to me. I got married when I was too young and I had three kids. I'm forty now and just look at me."

"You're still young," I told her. "You're still a pretty woman. I'm pretty, too, and who do you think I look like?"

"Me," she said and we laughed.

I hugged her and gave her a kiss.

"I love you, mom," I said. I remembered that when I was very young, I was the only one who could say nice things to her and make her smile.

Chapter Four

It was Friday evening and I was at my grandma's eating dinner.

My mom had given her an envelope from me with a little money in it I had tucked away for myself before my last rehab. I had never seen her so happy.

"How did you know?" she asked me. "I needed that money to pay the bills. They had almost cut our electricity off because we were so far behind, a couple months."

She was happy and I was laughing.

The phone rang.

"I'll get it, grandma," I said.

"It's probably your mom," she said.

I answered the phone and said hello and a man's voice said hello back to me.

"Who's this?" I asked.

"Did you forget me already?"

"I'd like to know who this is," I said.

"You can't recognize my voice?" Christopher asked me.

I started laughing.

"What are you doing?" he asked me.

"I'm just visiting my grandma."

"I'm sorry if I'm interrupting you. I thought you might come into the city so we could do some things together. I want to show you around. Could you come down next Sunday? Maybe we could go to a show."

I told Christopher, "Let me think. I have to make some plans. Where can I call you in about thirty minutes?"

I was excited.

I told my grandmother it was Christopher and that I might go to New York the next Sunday to see him.

"Good," she said. "Enjoy yourself. It'll be nice weather. I used to go to New York a lot when I was growing up. That's the only place I could have a good time, even if I was just watching people. Everybody walked. A lot of the women dressed up just to go walking. They wore beautiful clothes. But not any more.

The new generations don't wear those kinds of clothes and I don't like the way girls look these days."

I didn't know what to say. I knew how I usually looked.

I was still excited, though, and I decided to call my mom.

"Mom, I'm going to New York Sunday to meet Christopher!" I said.

"Where's he going to take you?" She asked me.

"I don't know."

"Maybe you should come home before you go. You'll have to look good. I've got a few clothes in my closet, a few dresses I've never worn before. If you don't find one you like, we can go to the store. You don't have any dresses at all, do you? I'll help you pick out some shoes and a new dress. They'll match."

"Thanks, mom."

The next morning, Saturday, I stayed with my grandma until noon, and then left so that my mom and I could go shopping for the clothes I'd wear Sunday with Christopher.

He always dressed nicely and always wore a tie. He was short, but was a handsome guy.

I'm not very tall myself, but I told my mom I shouldn't wear high heels with him.

While we were shopping, my mom asked me if I really liked this man.

"Yeah, I do," I said. "He's fun, mom. You've got to meet him some day. You can come to New York with us some day and we can all go shopping together there."

"I'd love to," she said.

Christopher met me at the train station when I got into New York Sunday afternoon. I was surprise because he was wearing casual clothes, just jeans, but he looked good.

I walked up to him and he looked at me and said, "You look different."

"What's different?" I asked him.

"I don't know," he said.

My mom had bought me an expensive casual dress and I had shoes to match and a bag. I didn't like to carry a bag, but my mom made me. I had had my hair done and I thought I looked good.

He seemed excited about how I looked, but I asked him to tell me if there was anything wrong with the way I looked. I wanted to know.

"No, you look … how should I say it? You look just beautiful. C'mon," he said and grabbed my hand.

We walked up to the street and got into a cab.

"Are you hungry?" he asked.

"No, I had lunch before I left," I said.

"We could have lunch if you want before we do anything else. I don't want you to walk around hungry."

The energy he had was so different from other men I knew. He was so alive.

"Okay, the first thing we're going to do is to go to my apartment and I'll show you where I live. Any time you want to come to the city and stay or just come by and take a nap—whatever you want to do—you can come to my place."

We took the cab to his apartment on the east side. It was a new building, twenty floors high.

He could tell I was nervous and he took me hand and told me not to be nervous.

I told him I didn't like elevators. "I get dizzy," I said.

He told me the elevator wouldn't bother me if I didn't pay too much attention to it and he kept talking to me and talking to me until suddenly he said, "Well, here we are. It's fast, no? Are you still afraid?"

"No, no. I'm okay," I said.

He opened the door to his apartment. The living room was like something you'd see in a movie, so well decorated. Everything matched. It was neat as a pin and so clean.

"Have a seat," he said and I sat on a couch that felt so good to me that I told him it would put me to sleep.

"It's so comfortable," I said to him. I told him I wanted to use his bathroom and he showed me where it was. It was sparkling clean too and everything was neat as a pin.

"How long have you lived here," I asked him.

"Five years, ever since I got a job in New York. It's a nice building and it's convenient. My office isn't far from here. Do you want something to drink?"

"Yes, just water though."

He got a little cushion for me and he told me to put my feet up, lay back and relax. He made himself some coffee and came back in and sat down next to me.

"Have you thought about what you'd like to do today? I can show you around. We could go on a boat. Do you like boats?"

"Yes, very much," I told him.

"People from all over the world take the boats on the Circle Line around the city. Have you ever gone on them?"

"No," I said.

"Then that's what we're going to do."

He asked me if I wanted to take a nap before we went and I told him no, I'd slept well the night before.

He told me he had to make reservations for dinner that night and I could choose whatever kind of restaurant I wanted. He took a number of menus from a drawer and brought them over to me.

"I don't cook," he explained. "I always go out or do take out."

I realized he had been carefully planning all this since we had talked on the phone.

As we rode over to the Circle Line in a cab, I told him that I didn't want to be personal, but I asked him if he had ever been married. "You're older than I and you act like you know how to take care of things in your apartment there. It looks so neat. It almost looks like nobody lives here. When I saw the Jacuzzi in your bathroom, I just wanted to jump in and soak myself. I've never seen a place like yours, that's so organized, in my life."

"Well, I'm by myself and have no kids, so maybe that's why it's so neat," he said.

"Did you ever get married?" I asked again.

"No. I was serious about one girl. We had gone to college together, but when we graduated, we went our separate ways. We've kept in touch by letter and phone, and she came to visit me a few times. It was what you call a long distance relationship, but it didn't work well. She works in Milwaukee with her father, a well known man, and they're much richer than I am. Her family wanted her to be together with them and she would never come here for more than a couple days and then she'd rush back home. While she was here, she'd call her mother or her brother I don't know how many times a day. If I had wanted to settle down and get married to her, I would have had to have gone the way of her family, and that was too difficult for me. They're rich and I think her parents wanted her to get married to a man of her background. It hurt when I realized we could never get married."

"You had a broken heart?" I asked him.

He started laughing, and just shrugged his shoulders. I think he was embarrassed.

"Sometimes," I said to him, "when you're lonely, you can be impulsive."

"I know, Gina. When I first saw you, I thought you and that girl had a similar look. Blond hair, blue eyes. She was a little taller than I am, but she was a beautiful girl. I thought we were going to get married. I even gave her an engagement ring once, but she wrote me a "Dear John" letter and mailed the ring back to me."

"Where's the ring," I asked him.

"I didn't want to keep it, so I took it back to where I had bought it. Well, that's my story. I'll have to ask yours some other time, because we're here."

I had my sweater on because I thought it might be a little windy in the boat, but he told me I'd be fine. He said there was food and drink on the boat and they had entertainment too. Some interesting people rode the boat, he said, and I'd enjoy them.

He took my hand. "You're warm and I'm cold," he said. I told him his cold hands meant a warm heart, but that I probably had a cold heart. We laughed. We were starting to get along together.

He had the most beautiful teeth. I smoked and my teeth were yellow, so I never wanted to open my mouth and smile a lot with him.

When we stepped onto the boat, I couldn't believe how many people were there and I asked Christopher if we could get something to eat. I had gotten hungry.

We went over to a huge buffet they had. I took just a couple items because I didn't want to be impolite. I ate those and then, even though I was a little embarrassed, I went back and got some more.

The people on the boat were dressed nicely, some casually and some more formally. I heard people speaking French and Japanese and other languages I couldn't identify. We sat and watched the people walking back and forth along the front deck of the boat.

"I should have brought a camera," I said.

"Don't worry. I can buy one here," he said. He did and we took pictures of people on the boat and pictures of Long Island and the city.

"Are you going to go back home tonight?" he asked me at one point.

"I have to. I didn't bring anything with me because I had no plans to stay," I said. "My mom will be waiting for me. I don't care what time I get home, though."

I really liked his company.

He told me about his parents and about his growing up and said maybe we could go visit them someday in Paris. I said I didn't know about going on a plane that far because I had a stomach problem and couldn't fly easily for long distances, I didn't think.

"Well, one day we'll see," he said.

He always had something to talk about. He always had something to do. He always said "we."

"This is real life," I said to myself. Christopher was showing me what life was really like and how one could really live. I thought about myself and about what I had been doing to myself and I started to get sad.

I felt there was a reason this man had come along and into my life, but only God knew what that reason was.

My mind changed a lot that afternoon. About the way I felt. About the way I looked at myself. About the way I wanted to live my life.

All this was running through my head and I had been silent for a while, looking over the water at the New York skyline.

Christopher looked over at me and said, "You have a lot on your mind. I look in your eyes and sometimes you look so sad. Sometimes you look happy. I like to hang around with you, even though sometimes you seem that sad. You don't have to tell me why. I'll find out for myself. A little bit at a time. I'd like to be your friend. You can come use my place anytime. I'm hardly ever here. I work late and don't get home until late. Weekends I go to my office too for a few hours each day because I have so much work on my desk. I've been alone for a long time. I don't date. I spend all my time in my office, and I make them a lot of money, but I would really just like to make you happy."

He took my hair and pushed it back so he could see my face.

"If we start to see each other more," he told me, "I think I should buy a little car and then we can drive up into the country. You don't live that far from here. Maybe I can get one next week. Then I've got to go out of town for a week or two—I won't know for sure until I get back to work a week from Monday—but before I leave, I think we should see each other again."

We looked into each other's eyes for a moment.

"I'm enjoying myself," I said.

We rode around New York on the boat until the sun started to go down and turned more yellow and then orange. It was beautiful. It had become a little chilly, but it was beautiful.

He said he didn't want the day to end, and I didn't want to go home either, but I knew I really shouldn't get home too late.

Finally I told him that we should leave. I had to get home.

"Okay," he said.

We had taken quite a few pictures of our wonderful day.

We took a taxi from the boat and he said he would drop me off at Grand Central. He paid for the cab there and got out with me.

"You don't have to walk me to my train," I said to him, but he said he wanted to.

"Let me get some magazines to keep you busy on the train," he said and went over to a newsstand and told me to pick whatever magazines I wanted to read. I never bought magazines because they were too expensive. I took a Vogue and Harper's Bazaar, so I could see how the girls in the magazines were dressed.

I was happy and I gave him a big hug. Then I kissed him.

I could see how pleased he was by a little kiss.

"You call me or I'll call you," he said as I was getting on the train. "Don't say good-bye," he added, "Just say 'I'll see you later.'"

I fell asleep on the train and when I got home, my mom was still up. My brother was there and they were both waiting for me to get home. I went into the kitchen and told my mom I had gone to his apartment and told her how beautiful it was. I'd never seen anything like it. I told her all about our boat ride around the city.

"I forgot everything that was bothering me, mom," I said, "and you know what I was thinking? I was thinking that that was real life."

My mom looked at me. She seemed sad for just a second.

"Oh, Gina. I stopped by grandma's house this afternoon and picked up your mail." She pulled out six envelopes from her purse.

One was from Ruben and one was from his sister.

"This looks like an invitation, mom," I said. I opened it up. Ruben's sister, Juanita, was going to get married. I was happy for her because she had gone through so much when she was growing up.

I told my mom I didn't know if I should go to the wedding because I hadn't seen her for such a long time. I talked to Ruben every once in a while by phone and he had written me a few letters, too, but I wanted to see Juanita get married.

My mother said I should go. "People don't get married every day," she said. "They would love to see you."

"I bet Juanita's beautiful, ma. She had such beautiful skin, beautiful eyes, such dark hair. You met her, didn't you, ma?"

"She spent the night here a few times."

"I can't wait to see Ruben. Mom, I probably will have to go to Juanita's shower, too. And what should I buy her?"

"Buy her some house ware. You know, anything she can use in the kitchen."

"Could you go with me? Oh! By the way, Christopher is going to Europe for two weeks. He says I can stay in his place. What do you think, mom?"

"That sounds wonderful," she said.

"You know, mom, everything's falling in my lap. I feel different, too. Christopher is so different from any other man."

My mom told me she was happy for me.

"You know, mom, I'm always thinking, and I always pray before I go to bed. When I was down, I talked to my grandma a lot. I'd tell her I was depressed. Even when I was little, I would tell her that. She'd tell me to pray. 'It will make you feel good,' she'd say. She'd tell me to tell God what I wanted and that someday he would give me an answer, but I had to work hard and keep my word. She always made me happy when I wasn't feeling good or when I was worried, ma. Always. I still remember everything she said to me. Grandma's like an angel, isn't she? Do you think there are angels on the earth, ma?"

Chapter Five

The night before Christopher left on his business trip to Europe, I took a late train into New York and took a cab to his flat.

Christopher was still awake and I asked him if he had been waiting up for me.

"No," he said. "I had work to do. I just made myself some warm chocolate milk to drink. Do you want some? I'll warm it for you."

"Oh, no," I said. "That would be too sweet. Well, maybe I'll have some, but with just a little chocolate."

Christopher told me I looked happy tonight and went into the kitchen.

"Really?" I asked. I went into the kitchen and gave him a hug.

"You're the nicest guy," I told him.

I told him I felt a little sorry for him, though, and I wondered if I was the girl for him. He was too nice.

"What do you mean?" he asked me. "What's wrong?"

"I'm just telling you that I think you're too good for me. I don't think that I'm the person that you want to spend your life with. You're too good."

"Don't talk like that," he said. "What's wrong with you? If a relationship doesn't work out, that'll be okay. I like to have friends. And you're not my lover. You're my friend. I like it that way."

"Me, too," I said.

But I still felt sorry for him. As much as he had and as much as he did, he still seemed like a lost soul.

"Who's going to take you to the airport?" I asked.

"I have a company car with a driver," he said. "He'll take me."

"I won't see you tomorrow then. What time are you leaving?"

"Right after noon," he said. "I'll call you just before I leave." He gave me a hug. "I guess I'm worried about you being here by yourself."

"I'm a big girl," I said. "I've been around."

"Gina, I don't cook very much," he said, "but if you want to cook, I'll show you where everything is."

"You don't have to show me," I said. "Everything is going to be fine. Don't worry about me. I appreciate what you're doing for me. Thank you. I don't know what else to say."

He put his hand gently over my mouth to let me know he didn't want me to say any more. "You already said thank you. That's enough. Come. I'll show you in here. Remember, this was my office? I've moved everything into the other room and I've fixed a bed for you. This will be your own place and you can do whatever you want to do in this room. I always like my own bed and I thought you probably did too. There are sheets and towels here."

"I don't want you to worry about me," I told him. "I'm not a little kid."

"No," he said. "You are a little kid. "Sometimes I look at you and I just see a little girl."

"Are you joking?" I asked him.

"No. It's true. Sometimes."

"You know, I've never met anyone like you. I'm always telling my mom about you. I even asked her to come to New York with me sometime and we can all go out."

"Sure. Anytime. Maybe when I'm not here you can invite your mom to come stay and you can go to a show. You and your mom can always go around the corner for dinner or lunch, even breakfast," he said.

He had taken me to a restaurant not too far from where he lived. He went there all the time, he'd said, and it was his second home. Everybody knew him there and I could tell they liked taking good care of him.

Christopher told me I looked tired and said to go to bed if I wanted to. I did and I fell asleep immediately and slept right through until the next morning.

When I opened my eyes to the light of the next day, I thought at first I had just napped for a couple of hours. I looked at the clock, though, and saw it was five in the morning. I started to get up and realized I was still in my clothes from the night before. I had just come in, lay down and fallen asleep. I hadn't even washed my face or brushed my teeth.

I got up. Christopher was still sleeping, it seemed, so I went back to bed and closed my eyes again. When I woke up later, I could hear Christopher in the kitchen.

"I went in to your room last night," he said, as if he was making a confession, "and you looked so pretty lying there sleeping, just like a little girl. I just let you sleep. You can go back to sleep again now, if you want to."

"No, it's okay."

"I have to be in my office at nine o'clock," he said. "but I always go for a little walk when I get up. If you want to come with me, I'd like it. If you don't want to come with me, that's okay too. You can stay home. I'll be back in an hour. What would you like to eat this morning? We can go out to breakfast. Do you want to do that?"

"Okay. Do you mind?"

"No. I'm just going to go walk around Seaside Park first. I'll see you later."

After he left, I called my mom. She asked if I was okay and I told her I had fallen asleep the night before and slept through to nine this morning. When I woke up, I thought I was home in my own bedroom when I was a little girl.

I told her that Christopher had cleaned his office out and made it into my very own bedroom for me. I was relaxed with him, I said, and I didn't worry much when I was here.

"I slept so well," I said. "You know, I have a hard time sleeping usually. Say hello to my brother and tell grandma hello, too."

Christopher came back from his walk and said he was going to take a quick shower and put on his clothes.

"I'm fast," he said.

While he showered, I looked around. His dressing room was as neat as everything else and he had a lot of suits in his closet. He must have had a good job. He only had a couple pair of tennis shoes, but he had seven pairs of polished leather shoes for work. I counted them. All his shirts were back from the cleaners and they looked like they had been pressed perfectly.

He came out of the shower wrapped in a towel. Steam was rising from his body.

"You really take a hot shower, huh?" I said.

"I love a hot shower."

"It's not hard to burn yourself, you know."

"Oh, no. It feels good."

His hair was wet and he was dripping all over the floor. I asked him why he didn't just dry himself off first before he came out of the bathroom.

"Oh, my God," he said. "You're giving me orders already and you've only been her for one day."

"C'mon, let's go," he said after he'd dressed, and we left for the restaurant.

Outside he started walking so quickly I couldn't keep up.

"I know you walk fast. I can't walk that fast," I told him.

He slowed down and took my hand.

At the restaurant the waitress asked Christopher, "The usual?"

He nodded.

"And what would you like to have, honey?" she asked me.

She had seemed surprised when he came in with me and she tried not to stare at me, but I saw her looking anyhow. I don't think they'd ever seen him bring anyone with him before.

I ordered a cheese omelet with toast and some coffee. He had sausage and quarter pancakes. They were very small and I'd never seen any like them before.

"Do you want a taste?" he asked.

"Just give me one bite, please." I took a piece from his fork into my mouth. "They're crunchy. They're delicious."

"Do you cook?" he asked me.

"Yes, I do."

"Breakfast?"

"Yes. I cook for my brother when I'm home. Oh! I forgot to tell you. I have to go to a wedding next week in Trumbull. It's too bad you're not going to be around. You could have come with me."

"Hey, it's too bad you couldn't have come with me to Europe."

"We don't know each other that well," I said to him.

"We know each other," he interrupted.

"I know we know each other. I didn't mean that."

"You don't have to explain," he said. "You know, when I was growing up, my parents told me I couldn't go near a girl unless I married her."

I didn't say anything to him. I just looked at him.

"You are old fashioned," I said.

"Yes, I am," he said. "That's how my parents taught me."

I suddenly wanted to change the subject. "This is a really good breakfast," I said. "The way they cook the eggs is great. It's like they browned them. That's how I like my eggs. Some day I'll can cook some at home for you."

"If I'm at home alone, I don't like to eat by myself. That's why I go out to a restaurant. I can see some people while I'm eating. If I eat by myself at home, I have no appetite."

"How long have you been living this way?" I asked him.

"Since I broke up with that girlfriend three years ago."

He still cared for that girl. I just reminded him of her. That was the way it was. But he was still a nice guy to be with.

After breakfast we went home and watched the news. I was sitting next to him on the couch and I held his hand. He put his arm around me and then kissed me on my forehead and my face.

"You know, Gina," he said, "you can tell me what's bothering you. I'd like to know., and sometimes it's good to talk about it. If you get it out, you'll feel better."

"The only thing bothering me now is how I'm going to pick out a dress for this wedding," I joked. I didn't want to tell him any more about myself yet

"I'm pretty good at picking out dresses," Christopher said. "Why don't I go into work late today. I know some good places to go. I used to go shopping with my girlfriend when she came to New York. Are you looking for a gown or a long dress or a short dress?"

"My mom says I should stick to a short dress that comes to my knees and that's open a little in the back maybe. She told me just not to get a black dress."

"I know a place," he said.

I was so happy that I didn't have to go alone because I had never bought any clothes for myself. I had no idea what to look for.

He pulled me up off the sofa and said, "C'mon! But we've got to hurry."

We took a cab across town to a little boutique and he picked out a dress that was a light green satin and moved perfectly when I walked. Then he took me to a shoe store and picked up a pair of shoes and a matching purse. I was all set for the wedding.

"Thank you," I said.

On the way home we stopped for coffee in a little Italian pastry shop. Just looking at all the different cheesecakes, layer cakes and pastries made me hungry. Christopher told me he came here once in a while. He said it was his favorite place for treats, but he got fat easily and that's why he jogged.

"You should go jogging too," he said, "because it makes you feel good."

I looked over at him. He did know how to live.

"Now I have to go to work," he said and we left, got a cab and he dropped me off at his apartment on his way to his office.

I put away all my new things and then washed my face and looked in the mirror. My face had been so dark around my eyes. Now there were shadows anymore. I was finally rested. I had been eating well. I hadn't been worrying.

Maybe I was happy.

Juanita lived in Trumbull now. I was surprised to find their house was a brand new one with a big yard. I went up and knocked on the door.

In a minute Juanita herself opened it.

"Oh, my God. You're so beautiful," I said to her. "Who's the lucky guy?"

"You've got to meet him."

Ruben came in to the room, said hello and shook my hand.

"How are you?" he asked. He seemed so formal.

"Oh, God," was all that I could say.

He relaxed a bit and then hugged me.

He was tall and he had turned out to be a handsome guy.

"And you turned out to be so beautiful," their mother said to me as she came into the front room. "You're such a pretty girl."

She hugged and kissed me.

"Have a seat," she said. "We have a lot to talk about."

"I need bridesmaids," Juanita said. "I need two girls. I think you should be one. Will you be?"

"Oh, sure. What do I have to do?" I asked her.

"It's easy. You'll be perfect."

She was so thrilled.

"Are you going to stay around for awhile?" her mother asked.

"Yes, for the weekend," I said.

"Why don't you stay for dinner?" her mother asked me.

"I don't know. Let me call my mom and see what she's doing. I was supposed to be getting together with her. My brother is home."

"How are they doing?" Juanita's mother asked.

"Fine."

"Let me show you around," their mother said.

She and Ruben showed me their house. Upstairs they had four big bedrooms. Downstairs they had walk in closets.

Ruben and I went outside and walked around. Everyone seemed to understand that we needed to be by ourselves. Ruben told me he and his two brothers had built the house themselves. It had taken them two years to finish it.

"Wow," I said. "I give you a lot of credit. It's beautiful."

"Thanks. I've been busy. This house took a long time to put together. It's still not done. We need to sort out the garage and cellar. I need the cellar because I work at home sometimes. I'm an accountant now. I actually got a college degree. Can you believe it?"

"I can, but, Ruben, I'm still on the edge sometimes, even though I've quit drinking. I haven't touched a drink in a year now. Or taken any drugs."

"That's good, Gina. Are you dating?"

"Yes, I have a friend. How about you?"

"No, I sort of had a girl, but no one really serious. I always have things to do and I want to make my mom happy. I feel like I still owe her. You know what I'm trying to say?"

"I think so," I said. He still felt like he had to be the man of the house.

I told him I never had graduated from high school.

"You could always go back to school," he said. "I did. You could too. If you wanted to."

"You've changed a lot. When we were together, all we wanted to do was have fun and smoke grass."

"I remember," he said. "We didn't know what we were doing."

"You're right," I said to him.

We walked down the street and around the neighborhood and I told Ruben how glad I was to see him again. I told him so many things had happened to me since I had seen him. Too many things. I couldn't pick myself up, I told him.

"My parents had moved to Derby, where they had built a house," I said. "Everything was nice at first. We had a swimming pool. We had animals, all kinds of animals. I had a dog too. It was like the country out there. My parents' marriage was breaking up though. My brother was not right. He'd become sick, mentally. Then my daddy died. I went down and down after that and I got very heavily into drugs. I even sold drugs. I went to jail. Many times. I didn't care about anything and I didn't want to know anything. All I wanted was drugs. Only my grandma paid any attention to me. Nobody could control me. Nobody could handle me."

Ruben had stopped walking and was just listening to me.

"My mother had been to a psychiatrist who had told her that she and I shouldn't talk. So she always hung up in the middle of our phone calls. She didn't want to hear from me. She didn't want anything to do with me. 'Let her just stay out there if that's what she wants,' the psychiatrist had told my mother. 'Don't bring her home.' My mother did everything that the psychiatrist told her to do. He had no mercy. Neither of them did."

"I really didn't know what to do with myself. I was living in the street and sleeping on the street. I'd go around the back corner of one restaurant, where the exhaust fan kept the concrete warm, to sleep, and in the morning I'd get up and walk around in the streets. People would pass me by and never even look at me. Nobody would have anything to do with me."

"I started begging my mom and told her I would do anything that she said, but I figured that she hated me by then because I had promised her so many times that I would straighten myself out, but I never did. I never listened to her.

You know, when you're into drugs, you're sick. You're evil. Every time my mother tried to get me help and put me somewhere, I would always run away. I'd end up in the streets. No one seems to know that when you do drugs and alcohol, you're not yourself anymore. The drugs take over your mind and your body. You have no soul. I even tried to kill myself. It didn't work. I just ended up in the hospital."

I looked over and saw Ruben crying.

"I'm very sorry," he said, "very sorry about what happened to you."

I remembered his brother had been doing heavy drugs for a long time too.

"When you're young, you don't know what you're getting into," I said. "It's like you can't tell the good from the bad and then, when you're addicted, it's too difficult to get back out."

Ruben hugged me.

I had started crying too.

"We'd better go," I said finally. "You're mom's waiting for us."

Ruben didn't talk much on the way home.

Finally he looked over at me. "I don't know what to say, Gina."

"Well," I said, "It's the past now. It's over. Now I have a new life. I met this man. He's very nice. He left a few days ago on a business trip to Europe. He'll be back in a couple weeks. Everything's good now, Ruben."

He said he was happy for me.

"I'm so glad that your sister is getting married," I said.

"Me too. He's a nice man and Juanita's very happy."

"She turned out to be so pretty," I said. "Ruben, we should get together, just you and I, while I'm around. We could go have dinner in some quiet little place. I would like that."

When we got back to his house, his mother had cooked roast beef. One of his brothers was there and he was a handsome man too. The other brother, the addict, lived somewhere else, but the younger brother still lived with his mother and Ruben did too. He stayed there because he still felt bad for her.

At dinner Ruben sat next to me. We all were drinking water except for Ruben's brother, who was drinking wine. He asked if I wanted some and I told him "No, thank you. I have to drive home."

Later, when I drove away, Ruben stood there and watched me go.

I had such mixed feelings about Ruben. About all of them, I guess. When we were little, we all used to chase each other and run and play all the time. We were innocent. We were having fun. It was weird that I was seeing them all again after all that had happened to me. I wished I were innocent again.

I went home and told my mom that I had had a good time, though.

"You know," she said, "your Christopher called and he said he'd call you back tomorrow. He sounds like a very nice man."

My mom paused and looked at me for a second.

"You look sad," she said.

"You know, mom, I am. Ruben's such a nice man now and he has a good job. You should see their house. Before I left Ruben walked me to the car, closed my door and just watched me as I drove off. I watched him in my rear view mirror. I felt like going back and giving him a big hug and holding him in my arms and kissing him."

"You could be friends. He could be, you know, a good friend. It's different with girls. Sometimes you just don't see them anymore, but with guys you can be long term friends."

Chapter Six

Ruben called me the next morning.

"Hey, guess what I found?" he asked. "A picture of you and I. I think my mom took it. We were little, and we're kind of holding hands. It's cute. I'd like to take you out to dinner tomorrow night, if you have nothing else to do"

"Sure!" I said. "Come over to my house and we'll go from there."

"We don't have to hang around this town," he said. "We'll go to Westport. They have a lot of good restaurants there."

"Good. I'll be ready."

"What time do you want me to come over?"

"Is seven okay?" I asked.

"That's fine. I'll be there," he said. He sounded happy.

On the way to the restaurant I started talking about our past.

"Remember? My mom threw me out of my house and I ran away from my aunt's too and stayed with your mom for a while? My father came by one night and pointed a gun at you. I didn't know he'd do that. And it went off. I felt so sorry for you. He got arrested."

"And he wasn't the only one who did," Ruben said and laughed. "Remember our trip to Florida?"

I did, but I had been thinking of Ruben when he was eight years old.

When we got to the restaurant, Ruben opened the car door for me, and we went in to eat. It was a nice, quiet little place.

"When I just want some peace and quiet and to be myself for awhile, I come here," Ruben said. "What do you like to eat?"

"Anything. What's good here?" I asked.

"I like the grilled chicken."

"Maybe I'll order a steak," I said.

He took an old, crumpled snapshot out of his pocket and showed it to me.

"Oh, my God!" I said. "I was so fat!"

"Yeah, you were a little chubby. But you look good now."

"And look at my hair! It was so greasy."

"But you looked good," Ruben said. "You still do."

After we had eaten, Ruben started opening up to me. There was no more of that first formality I had seen. We were chatting like two twelve year olds planning to go to the park.

"After I got out of jail, I didn't smoke grass anymore and I didn't drink anymore and I didn't steal cars," he told me. "I realized I didn't want to be like my dad, and I had become just like him. My mom didn't need that. She didn't need one more man like him in her life. Somehow I had become like him after he died."

I suddenly felt bad that I hadn't seen Ruben for so long.

"Now I work long hours," he said. "Maybe I should slow down. I had met a lot of girls when I went to school, but at that time I really didn't want to date because I didn't want to be distracted. I knew that to have a girlfriend, I had to spend time with her, and if I couldn't spend time with her, the relationship wouldn't work. So I didn't date."

"Maybe you can now because you're grown and you've finished all you've been trying to do," I said to him.

"Once I got hurt too, although I really just hurt myself," Ruben went on. "I met one girl who I had had my eyes on. I would talk to her from time to time at college and one day we walked out of class and I introduced myself and she told me her name, Julia. I was kind of shy. I didn't talk easily to strangers, especially a pretty girl, but we talked from time to time. When I asked her for a date, she said no. I went home and told my mom about her. My mom tried to make me feel better by telling me that sometimes a girl wouldn't say yes right away. "They like to take their time and they like to get to know you sometimes," she said. 'She may be too busy, like you. But keep asking her. That's okay.' My ma always made me feel good. She's a saint. Or at least an angel. I didn't bother the girl for a while, but one day I bumped into her in the hall at school. I told her I really wanted to get together with her when she felt she had some free time. She said no again. I told my mom maybe she just didn't like me or that maybe I wasn't good enough for her. My mom said not to give up if I really liked her. One day I stopped and bought her flowers, but that day I didn't see her, so I brought them home to my mom. My mother felt sorry for me, but she told me not to worry. 'That girl just likes to be chased,' she said. Then one day I was walking around the bookstore and bumped into her there. We started to talk and I asked her what she liked to read. There was a coffee bar in the bookstore and I invited her to sit down with me if she had a little time. She said sure. We sat down and continued talking. I asked her for her phone number and gave her mine and said we should get together for dinner sometime. The next time I saw her in school, we started talking again. 'I told you,' my mom said. Julia and I began to meet and share our homework. She was studying psychology and she hated numbers. I told her I could teach her numbers, but mostly we talked about psychology. We became even closer."

"Then I just stopped seeing her. I had too much going on, but I think I was also kind of afraid to get involved. Maybe she'd dump me. So I dumped myself first. I still call her, though. Hey! I'm doing all the talking, Gina. How about you?"

"My life … maybe I'm not strong enough. Sometimes I'm still afraid. I'm afraid of myself. I never know what I will do next. I'm afraid to get really serious with anybody. I told you my life is on the edge. I'm not sure about anything a lot of the time. I have to straighten myself out still."

The next day I was back at Ruben's, but Ruben looked upset, although I could tell he was trying to control it. There were so many people in the house, I said to him, "Why don't we go for a little ride down to the beach? We always went to the beach when we were little."

"I have to get up early tomorrow morning," Ruben said, "and arrange a funeral for my brother. He was killed last night in a drug deal gone bad. I knew for a long time that something like this was going to happen. I kept telling him, but he wouldn't listen to me. I was tired just from being around him. For so many years I did so much for him. I couldn't do anymore. I'd decided I was just going to let him go. I had spent so much money on him, so much time. My mom had, too, my sister had, everybody had."

Ruben's eyes were red with tears and I felt like mine were too.

"I don't understand why every time I tried to get him help, he never wanted to get help. He thought he knew everything. He wouldn't listen to anyone."

I told Ruben that I had done that too.

"There were not many people like my brother," Ruben said. "He had been taking so many drugs, heroin, cocaine, LSD. Whenever I had run into him, his arm was black and blue from injecting. I would get so mad at him. One night my brother came up to me—he was on drugs—and started screaming at me that I was a murderer. I had killed the only dad he had ever had. I started punching him and I went completely out of control. He was too stoned to defend himself. The next day his face was all swollen and I felt so sorry. I told my mother what happened. She said God would forgive me."

Ruben stopped talking and seemed to be thinking about all he had just said.

"Gina," he said, "you remember that time I went to jail after I stole that car? When I came home from jail, I changed. But I had done a terrible thing when I killed my father. That's still on my mind. It always will be."

"You're a strong man, Ruben," I told him. "Whatever you want to do, you're free now. You don't have to worry about your brother anymore. Your sister's married. She's going to be moving out. Only your little brother and mother are still at home, and he's about to move out, too. He's grown up. You can sleep easily now. You won't have to worry about your phone ringing in the middle of the night and hearing a policeman or a doctor telling you they have your brother. You can live in peace now."

Ruben was crying. He still couldn't believe what had happened to his brother.

"Gina, I just don't understand people who don't want to quit. I told him if he had to do drugs, at least do them in moderation. He just didn't know how to do that. He always had to go all the way."

When we got home, Ruben invited me in for a minute before he took me home. I shouldn't drive myself, he said. It was too late. I told him no, he had to stay home in case any of his relatives who were staying there needed him.

"You'd better get some sleep," I said to Ruben, "because tomorrow you have to bury your brother. I'll come by early in the morning to help you, shop or get stuff, whatever you want. I'll just be here first thing tomorrow morning. See you then."

When Ruben walked me out to the car, I saw he was shaking and sweating. It was warm out still, and as I drove home I was feeling so sorry for him and I kept crying as I drove. I pulled over for a minute to wipe my eyes and calm down, and then I drove the rest of the way home.

My mom had already gone to sleep so I went straight up to my room and got in bed.

I couldn't close my eyes. I had a headache. I was upset and I wanted something so badly to stop my pain. I didn't even know if I could pray.

I thought of one friend who had been taking drugs for a long time. When I hung around with him, all we would do was shoot cocaine and drink. He finally overdid it too.

I had called him one night and there was no answer. I called his parents and he wasn't there either.

I called my mom and told her I had looked all around for Jim, but I couldn't find him. I asked her to go with me to his house. I thought something might be wrong because he never went out. He always answered the phone when I called at night.

It was so late that my mom said she wasn't going to drive me over here.

The next morning I got up early and went over to his house. Nobody opened the door when I knocked, but his car was parked outside. I knew he was in there.

I pushed on the door and it was unlocked so I walked in. I saw him lying in the bathtub. Blood was still coming out of his nose and his ears. His guts were all pushed out.

I called the police and waited outside until they arrived.

The police asked me questions and I said I was not here whenever it happened. I had only just come by this morning.

The cop told me he had overdosed. Too much cocaine killed him, the policeman told me.

After I left Jim's house, I didn't know what to do. I just walked around for a long time that day. I didn't feel like myself for a long time after that either.

My mom told me that if I didn't take care of myself, I was going to end up like him too.

Whenever I thought of finding Jim, I would shudder and feel nauseous and I stayed sad for days. Finally I started drinking vodka straight to ease my pain and make me forget what I kept seeing in my mind, Jim floating in the bathtub.

Then I did more drugs.

The next morning I went to Ruben's early. Just after I got there, Juanita came into the house screaming and crying.

I told her how sorry I was about her brother and I hugged her and gave her a kiss on the cheek. She was beside herself still. Finally she managed to sit down in a chair. It was so sad.

The rest of her family was sobbing too. Many were drinking, even though it was still early in the morning. I wanted to start drinking with them, but I didn't.

I asked Ruben if he was okay and he told me he was, but it didn't look like he had slept at all. I told him he should sit down with me for a minute and we'd have a cup of coffee. I asked if he wanted me to make him breakfast.

His mother was trying to tend to her company and I helped her set the table for them all. I offered to go get some groceries if she needed them, and his mother gave me a grocery list. Ruben said he'd go with me.

All the way to the store Ruben kept telling me how sorry he felt for his sister.

When we got back home, I played with one of his nieces and one nephew. There were a lot of kids still arriving with their parents and I finally took them all outside and we played ball and threw a Frisbee.

After we came back in, I got plates of food for them and sat them down at the table to eat.

Ruben had been watching me.

"Thank you very much," he said. "I really appreciate what you're doing. You look good with those kids, too."

I did love kids.

Everyone there was feeling very badly and no one was acting normally, especially Ruben's mother. His sister and his little brother were just trying to help out now.

"I don't think we should bury him today," Ruben said to me early that afternoon, "because no one is ready. We'll do it tomorrow. If you're tired, you can go lie down. You've done a lot. Go into my room, lay down and take a nap."

"No, thanks. I've got to go home and check on my own mom. She might need me to do something for my brother. He's not too good today."

"Maybe I'll see you tomorrow," Ruben said.

"I am coming tomorrow," I told him.

I went home and my mom and I made lasagna and pepper steak to bring to Ruben's mom the next day.

The next afternoon we were all sitting down outside at Ruben's eating a meal before the wedding ceremony. Ruben was serving the drinks. Even though he was feeling badly, he had managed to organize everything for the dinner and to take care of all the guests.

He, his mother, sister and brother had held a spur of the moment burial service at the cemetery that morning. They didn't want anyone else there. They wanted to keep everyone's attention on the wedding as much as possible.

I was sitting at one table and Ruben was walking around, tending to people, when a beautiful girl walked into the yard. Ruben looked at her and I could see the surprise on his face.

The girl went over to him and Ruben kissed her.

"Hello, Julia," he said.

They hugged each other tightly. Ruben's face suddenly looked happy. I just watched.

Juanita leaned over to me then and told me she was Ruben's girlfriend. They hadn't seen each other for a long time, but they'd known each other for years, Juanita said.

My heart dropped. I realized I was jealous. I still had feelings for Ruben, but I was happy for him too because this girl had come back into his arms. He looked happy.

I watched them together and I saw they were walking toward where I was sitting and I realized Ruben was going to introduce her to me.

"Gina, this is Julia, my friend I told you about."

"Pleased to meet you," I said.

Ruben asked her to have a seat and she sat down next to Juanita.

Everyone had been eating, but they all stopped and looked Julia. She was a beautiful girl.

She had the same color hair as I did. Her skin was light. She was thin. She looked a little younger than Ruben. I thought she must have a good job because she had pulled up in a BMW. Her dress, her hair, her makeup were all perfect.

I was glad for Ruben. He looked different now that she was here.

Even so, it was a long day.

That night I told Ruben my mother and I had come in the same car, and we were about to leave. It was late.

"I can imagine you're very tired," he said. "Thank you for everything."

He walked my mother and me outside and pulled me aside.

"I've been so happy to see you. You've made me very happy."

"Ruben, I was happy to see you too. Your girlfriend's a beautiful girl."

He said thank you, but I could see he really didn't know what to say.

I told him I'd see him the next day. My mother and I got in the car and he leaned over and kissed me through the window.

"Good night, Gina. Drive carefully," he said.

On the way home I told my mom I was glad his girlfriend had come back. He looked so different after she arrived, I said.

Juanita called me once after the wedding and I asked her to say hello to everybody for me. I would write them all when I could, I said.

I got together with Ruben once after the funeral, too. We sat having a coffee together and he told me how bad he felt that everyone was sad for Juanita's wedding. I told him not to feel bad. It was life. It could have been worse.

"I don't understand why life is so hard," he said. "There's always some tragedy."

"You can't have good without bad, Ruben, but you have to think of your own life from now on. Marry that girl. You two look good together. I watched you."

Ruben was looking at me and his eyes were sad. I saw that he still had feelings for me, too.

I told him to call me whenever he wanted to talk to me or see me and kissed him good-bye.

I was so glad I had my mom to go home to because if I had been alone, I would have found some drugs to take.

When I got home, I told my mom that Ruben's brother had been taking drugs for a long time and had been part of a gang. He must have owed them drugs or money, I said, and the gang members had killed him. Those guys were like that.

I knew.

That night I did pray.

The next morning I took off again for New York and Christopher's. I felt like I was going from one life to another.

Chapter Seven

Christopher called me at his place from Europe and asked me how I was doing, how everything was going. He missed me, he said.

I just told him that the wedding had gone beautifully and the dress that he had gotten me was perfect. Everybody loved it. My hair was up and I wore large earrings and a necklace, just like he'd suggested.

He didn't need to know anything about Ruben's brother.

I told Christopher I couldn't wait for him to get home. He said he was going to take a few more days while he was there and go visit his parents.

I told him I missed him, and he said maybe he wouldn't go see his parents, but I insisted he see them while he was there. I was sad that he'd be gone another week, though.

He heard the sadness in my voice and asked me what was wrong.

"Everything's fine," I told him.

"No, it's not. I know your voice, when you're happy and when you're sad."

"No, there's nothing wrong. I just can't wait for you to come home."

I still felt sad for Juanita, too. Every wedding anniversary she would have, she would also have the nightmare of her brother's death.

Christopher said he had been trying to reach me at my mom's and grandma's, but no one had answered the phone. He was afraid something had happened to me.

I told him everything was fine. We'd just been at Juanita's a lot.

"I'll see you one week from tonight at about eight," he said. "I can't wait. We can go out to dinner."

I thought I could make it a week.

The morning of his return I got up early and went out and got my hair and nails done. I went home and took a long nap, all afternoon. I felt I was still exhausted from the wedding.

When I woke up, I thought Christopher might be too tired to go out and eat. I decided to go to the grocery store and get some fresh things so I could cook dinner for him.

When Christopher came in around eight-thirty that night, I started to hug and kiss him, but he asked me what that smell was.

"Bad or good smell?" I asked. I wondered if it was me.

"Smells good. You're making dinner!? What is it?"

"Roast beef. I've got onions, carrots, tomatoes and potatoes too. I cooked them together in a side pot."

"I haven't had a home cooked meal … forever. Even my parents just took me out to eat last week."

"Cooking takes time."

"I'm starving too. I haven't eaten all day because I've been running since I got up. I almost didn't make my plane. I ran all the way. After I settled in my seat, I realized I was exhausted and I fell asleep for most of the flight."

He walked around the house and went into the bathroom and then came out and said everything was in such good order. Hadn't I stayed here, he asked.

I told him I came by a few times, but mostly I had been in Connecticut for the wedding. I told him he could see pictures of me in the dress he had gotten when they mailed me the photos they'd taken.

"Come over here," he said. "Let me look at you now. You changed your hair a little bit."

"Just a little trim. I thought it was too long."

"No, it wasn't. You look very pretty in long hair. All went well at the wedding?"

"Yes, I had a good time. How about you?"

"Everything's fine. My uncle just retired. Usually I go hunting with him, but this time I just stopped by for a couple hours. I spent most of the time with my mom. I'll have a vacation coming up sometime soon and I'm going to take it with them. I wish you could come with me."

We sat down for dinner and I asked him what he wanted to drink.

"Water." He didn't have any wine or liquor or even wine glasses in his place. I don't think he had ever entertained. I was going to have him cut the meat, but I realized he may never have done that, so I cut it myself and served him.

"This looks so good," he said.

"I hope it tastes 'so good,'" I said.

He took a large bite.

"It's delicious," he said.

"You're just hungry," I said.

He wanted to know all about Connecticut and so I told him about the wedding and how I had dressed up for it, but I didn't say anything about the funeral.

I showed him the jewelry I'd bought, just as he recommended. He asked if it was expensive and I said no, it was fake.

"Maybe we should have spent more time before I left getting some other jewelry for you," he said. "A girl should get gifts. She shouldn't have to buy her own jewelry."

He told me his mother had loved to cook him roast beef when he was little and asked if I had known that roast beef was his favorite meal.

"I didn't know that," I said.

"I feel like you've been talking to my mom," he said. "Thank you for dinner. I enjoyed it." He gave me a little kiss.

I started to clean off the table and he told me to go sit down and relax. I went in and sat on the sofa and he sat down next to me.

"I missed you when I was in Europe. I should have brought you, but I was running around so much for work I couldn't have been with you much anyway. Nevertheless, I feel bad that I left you here."

"Don't worry about me. I had stuff to do. I was okay, but I missed you too."

He got up and went and unpacked his suitcase. He had brought me a present in France, he said, and he came back in and gave it to me.

"I went shopping with my mom and she told me a girl likes pearls. I don't know if you like them or not."

I opened the box and there was a beautiful string of huge pearls. They looked very expensive to me. When I put the necklace on, I saw there were matching earrings in the box underneath. I put them on too. They were beautiful.

"You shouldn't have bought these pearls for me. They're too expensive. They are beautiful, though."

"You like them?"

"Like them? I love them. I've never had anything this beautiful." I hugged and kissed him and for the first time, he kissed me back.

I was crying, the pearls were so beautiful.

He asked me why I was crying and I told him I had never had anything like this before.

"I don't know why you spent so much money."

"You deserve it. My mom says you can wear pearls with anything. A suit. A dress. A blouse even."

"Thank you," I said and I started crying again.

"Don't cry," he said.

"I'm not crying sad. I'm crying happy."

"Oh," he said.

He hugged me again.

"Can I go clean the dishes now?" I asked. I was too embarrassed to stay with him.

"Sure," he said.

He went and took a shower and I thought about how wonderful he was. He knew how to make me happy and I liked to have him near me.

When he came out of the shower, he said to me, "I was thinking maybe after I go into the office tomorrow, I'll take some days off from work. I could rent a car and we could go drive around in the country."

My father had always taken me for rides in his car on Saturday afternoons when I was a little girl. I couldn't wait to go with Christopher.

Christopher asked me if I were going to bed. I said I had bought a book and I was going to read for a while if I couldn't get to sleep. I told him that sometimes if I read only two or three pages, I'd be asleep. A book was like a tranquilizer for me. I would never finish reading a book, I told him.

Christopher said he seldom read now. He just brought his work home and that made him tired.

"Do you want me to come in and tuck you in?" he asked.

"Sure."

I changed into my pajamas, but left my socks on because it was a little chilly.

Christopher came in before I had crawled under the sheets and asked me if I always slept with my socks on.

"Is it that cold in here?" he wanted to know.

"I'm just cold blooded," I told him, "like a little snake."

He went to the closet where the extra blankets were and handed me one that was thick and warm. He helped me put it on the bed and then told me, "Get in," as if I were a little kid.

I got in.

"I feel good when you're here," he said, "because I've been alone so long. Now I have someone to come home to. When you're not here, I don't bother coming home until late. I just go to the restaurant and then walk around a little. Now I can't wait to come home after work. Why don't you meet me for lunch tomorrow? I go to lunch at twelve thirty. We can go to that little restaurant, my favorite, that we've been to a couple of times. It's not far from here."

"Sure."

He kissed me on my forehead and gave me a little hug.

"I've got to be in the office at six tomorrow morning. I hope I won't wake you up."

"Six?" I said. "Go to bed. I'll see you in the morning."

"Thank you for dinner. I didn't even know you could cook."

"My grandma taught me."

I got up around ten the next morning. I had been so comfortable and so warm.

I made my bed and went in to make his bed, but he'd already made it. I took all the dirty clothes off his chair and dropped them off at the cleaners on my way to meet him for lunch.

The little restaurant was very busy.

I had put on just a pair of jeans and a simple blouse, but I was wearing the pearls. They looked good and I had the earrings on too.

As soon as Christopher saw me he said, "My mom has good taste, huh?"

He sat down and held my hand. "Are you okay?" he asked. "You look a little sad."

I knew I was still down after Ruben's brother's funeral.

"Maybe that's just my nature," I told him. I still wouldn't tell him about Ruben's brother. When I talked to Christopher, I always felt I had to think for a moment before I said anything. I had so much I didn't want to say.

We ordered and ate. I ordered a cheeseburger, and the meat was so soft it melted in my mouth. I refused dessert because I knew I would gain weight so easily.

I told him I had dropped off his laundry at the cleaners and he told me I didn't have to do that. I said I liked to work around his house.

"I don't want you to cook tonight. What you did last night was great, but tonight I want to take you out to dinner."

That night we went to a Japanese restaurant and we had out own private room.

"Bear with me, Gina," Christopher said after we had settled down on our pillows. "I didn't even ask you if you liked Japanese food or not."

"This is fine. I eat any kind of food. This is wonderful, our own little private room. It's very romantic. Cozy."

"I love Japanese food," Christopher said. "I'm not too good with fried food or greasy food, so I like Japanese cooking because they don't use too much oil. My stomach can't take much fried food. If I eat it, I can't go to sleep. When you live by yourself, that's no fun. Now I have you to come home to. That makes me happy."

I suddenly got nervous. I was afraid he was about to ask me to marry him.

"We've been together for a while now. What do you think of me?" he asked.

"Christopher, if I didn't like you, I wouldn't be here with you."

His face lit up.

In so many ways he was a nice guy, but I always felt he was holding back, maybe even hiding something. Like me. He was affectionate, but then I thought maybe European men were different than American men. I didn't know. The first thing American men wanted to do with me was to jump into bed with me. Maybe European men were different, I thought.

"I've been with you for a while now, Christopher. You're different than other men."

"In what way?" he asked.

"You know, every time I go out with a man, the first thing he asks me is to take my clothes off."

"I told you the first time I met you that I take my time," he said. "I can't do it because of the way I was raised."

"Do you remember once you told me I looked like your girlfriend?"

"I never should have told you that. That was a mistake. Sometimes I say things too quickly and I talk before I think sometimes, Gina."

I sat there looking at him and thinking. I knew he had a broken heart. Sometimes a man with a broken heart will never trust another woman again. Yet if a man has a broken heart, he can also fall in love very easily.

I thought Christopher was a one woman man. When he liked someone, he settled on her for life.

"I just need someone," he said suddenly.

"What do you need?"

"Someone who's home. Someone I can look forward to coming home to."

He'd always want me to stay at home, I thought.

"Do you want to work outside the home?" he asked me.

Was he reading my mind?

"Not really. But I have to have some money in my pocket so I can do things for myself. I haven't worked for a while because I wasn't feeling too well."

"What happened?"

"It's a long story. Some day I'll tell you. It's personal, but it's nothing between us."

"You know, I travel a lot. In a month I have to go to Italy. Maybe you should come with me. There's a lot to see. Have you ever been there?"

"No."

"I've thought that maybe some day when I retire, I'll move to Italy. I go there a lot for my job, sometimes three times a year. I have to go to Greece and I like it there too, but I go all over. I need someone to be by my side. I need someone interested in what I'm doing. It's lonely traveling by myself."

"Are you sure it's me you want traveling with you?" I asked.

"I would love it. I make enough money for both of us. You wouldn't have to worry. Think about it. Travel is nice when you're young. When you're older and have kids, it's better not to travel."

I had no education. I had dropped out of school and never went back, never went to college. I had learned many things, but they were all the wrong things. I felt like I knew so much less than Christopher did.

If I left him, I'd go back to the life I'd had before. I'd been in rehab for ten months before I met him and I'd become serious about changing. For the first time I'd started doing something for myself. It was different now, even though sometimes my mind would start to take me into a direction I really didn't want to go.

Christopher was always keeping me busy. We always had things to do.

I started thinking about what he'd offered.

Chapter Eight

That next weekend he rented a car and we drove up to Bear Mountain State Park in upstate New York. We drove up to the top of the mountain and we could see far off across the Catskills. It was beautiful, but chilly and windy. We could see thunderstorms passing by on the horizon.

After we came back down the mountain, we stopped at a little German restaurant that looked like it had been there for years. We ordered different dishes and shared.

After lunch we drove around the countryside past lots of beautiful farms. Some of them had pastures with racehorses in them. After a while I started to get sleepy and Christopher told me to put my seat back so I could nap.

He pulled over, got out and came around to my seat and adjusted it so I could lay all the way back.

"There you are," he said. "You can take a nap."

I closed my eyes as he drove off and when I woke up, I thought I'd dozed for five or ten minutes, but I must have slept for two or three hours.

We were almost back in New York and it was getting dark. Christopher had driven so smoothly that I was completely relaxed in the car for the whole trip. As we went up to his condo, I told him how good a time I had had with him.

He had told me in the car that afternoon that his mother had taught him everything he knew about how to treat a girl. He wondered if it might have been bad for him to get so used to hanging around his mother when he was younger. He had felt lonely living by himself at college. After he graduated, he went right back home and lived with his parents.

His mom had told him to take a little rest before he started working because once he started, he'd never have time for a break again. She said that she and his dad had been happy to put him through college, but after he took a little break, it was time for him to start doing his own thing.

"You're a man now," she told him. "Not that I want to get rid of you," she added. "I love you too much."

Christopher told me he always felt secure at home because his parents had a good marriage. It was a solid home, he said, even if sometimes his mother over-protected him. When he finally did leave home for good, he was sad, he told me.

His mom had spoiled him in many ways, he said, even though she made him work when he was home by taking out the garbage, painting the outside, caring for the lawn.

"She really was trying to make me into a real man," he said and laughed.

One day he was sitting in the kitchen having coffee with her and she looked down at his hands.

"I've never seen hands like that," she told him. "Your dad's hands aren't like that. Your hands are so clean. There's no dirt smudged on them. Your nails are clean and cut perfectly."

"I'm not a farmer. I work in an office," he told her.

"Right, you push a pencil, not a hoe. It's good to dirty your hands, you know."

"Mom, I work in the middle of New York city," he said to her. "My father and I are very different. He really is a farmer."

"You've got fingers like a girl's," she said.

He told me that sometimes his mother would speak out like that without thinking. She didn't know how badly she could hurt his feelings.

He felt bad for a long time that his hands looked like a girl's.

My back was bothering me when we got home because I'd been sitting in the car all day long. I didn't say anything or complain, even though I had a hard time getting out of the car. I just told Christopher I was a little tired when we got upstairs.

I said I had eaten so much at lunch that I wasn't really hungry for any dinner. He said he was just going to get himself a little bite. I went in to my room, changed my clothes, then washed my face and brushed my teeth. I was ready for bed.

He said he had some work to do and I should just go ahead and go to bed if I wanted to. He told me not to get up early the next morning either and that he'd come in to check on me before he went to bed.

I snuggled into my bed and just lay there for a while, relaxing my back. It had never been right since my first motorcycle accident. I was almost asleep when he came in and asked me if I was all right. I told him I was just a little tired.

"You sat in the car a long time today. You're probably a little stiff," he said.

I didn't tell him how bad my back was.

He gave me a hug and kissed me good night.

I closed my eyes and the next thing I knew it was morning. I got up and went to the bathroom, but Christopher was still sleeping. A little while later I heard the front door close. He had gone out for a walk, I thought. I fell back asleep.

The next thing I knew I heard the front door again. He was back from a long walk. I got out of bed, but my back still ached.

"If you don't mind," I said to him, "I think I'm going to go and soak myself a little bit. My back's stiff, like you said. I've never sat in a car for that long before. We should do it more often so I can get used to it because I really enjoyed myself." I gave him a hug and kiss on the cheek.

When I went into the bathroom, I looked in the mirror and saw how good I looked. I had color in my face. My cheeks were actually pink. For so long I had looked pale and a little gray because I smoked so much. I looked down at my nails. They were no longer yellow from the cigarette smoke either.

Christopher didn't smoke and I had never let him see me smoke, so I had cut down to almost nothing since I had been with him. I could breathe better too. My hair looked and smelled better. And now I saw my skin actually had some color in it from our ride in the country the day before.

I made the water in the tub as hot as I could and when I eased in, it felt wonderful on my back.

Suddenly Christopher came in and asked if I needed help.

"You don't have everything you need," he said and reached in the cabinet. He brought a bottle over to the tub.

"What's that?" I asked.

"What you still need. Bubble bath." He poured it into the tub.

"I've never taken a bubble bath," I said.

"I used to take bubble baths when I was a kid. I never wanted to get out of the tub. I just wanted to play with the bubbles. If my mom tried to get me out, I'd start crying. Now turn around."

I turned around and he started washing my back.

"Your muscles are so tight," he said and began rubbing the muscles on my neck too. It felt good.

"That's what I need," I said.

"I get a massage from time to time," he said. "There's a girl who lives in this building who gives massages. Maybe you should call her. I've got the number. She could come up and give you a massage."

"Really? I've never had a massage either."

"You have to have one. When your muscles get tight, you need one."

"When can I get one?" I asked.

"Maybe later today. I'll call her."

He kept rubbing my back.

"Christopher, lean over," I said.

He leaned toward me and I reached around his neck and pulled him into the tub. He still had his shirt and pants on.

"You asked for it," I said. "Doesn't this feel good?"

"God, this water's so hot!" he said.

"Okay. Why don't you run some cold water in here?"

He ran a little bit and I told him "Not too much! I like it hot!"

We were laughing hard by that time.

"Let me wash your back now," I said. I took off his shirt. "God, your skin is softer than mine!"

I grabbed him and held him tightly while I kissed him.

"You feel good," I said.

I took his hand and guided it across my sensitive parts. I pulled his mouth to my face.

I don't think he had much experience being intimate. I had to help him take his pants off.

"My underwear, too?" he asked.

"Yes."

"That feels good," he said as I started caressing him.

We made love in the warm water.

He told me he loved me.

Afterward he told me the water was still too hot for him, and he was getting dizzy. We got out of the tub and he took a towel and dried me.

"Christopher, my back feels good now after your massage. Look. I can turn my neck now, too."

"Lie down," he said. "I can work on your back some more. I've been getting massages for a long time and I think I know how to do it."

I went and lay down on the bed and he started rubbing my back and my legs.

He asked me why my body was so stiff and I told him I had fallen in the snow a few times. I wouldn't tell him about any motorcycle accidents.

He put some cream on me and rubbed it into my muscles. I closed my eyes because it felt so relaxing.

"Christopher, I'm in heaven. Nobody has ever given me a massage like this in my whole life. You're wonderful." I pulled myself up and gave him a kiss and then hugged him tightly. "Lie down here with me."

We lay down together and I put my head on his chest. I felt so comfortable with him. So safe.

I fell asleep in his arms.

The next morning I woke up and could get out of bed quickly.

Usually I pulled myself out of bed slowly because my back was a little stiff in the morning. I walked around the room and I didn't feel anything. Usually my knee hurt me, too, when I first stood on it, but not this morning.

I went into the kitchen and started breakfast. I knew he liked bacon and eggs over easy, and when they were ready, I went to his bedroom door and called him. He didn't answer.

I looked into his room, but couldn't see him because he'd covered his head with his blanket. I tiptoed over and kissed his ear and whispered that I'd cooked him his favorite breakfast.

"What?" he said. "What time is it?"

"It's almost eleven."

"Oh, my God! I've never slept this late. What happened? I feel like I took a tranquilizer last night. I've never slept this long."

"That's good you relaxed. You must have needed it," I said.

"You said you already cooked my breakfast?"

"Yes."

"Okay. I'm getting up."

He put his arms around my neck and gave me a kiss.

"I think I'm going to call you 'tiger,'" he said.

"Why's that?"

He just smiled, but I'd never seen a smile quite like that on his face before.

He went into the bathroom, cleaned up and put on shorts and a shirt. He was always so polite. I was just in my tee shirt.

I poured his coffee and told him to pour his own milk because I didn't know how much he liked. I put his breakfast on the table and he looked for a second at his eggs and bacon.

"I feel like I'm at the restaurant. You really know how to cook," he said.

"I like to cook. I like to eat too."

I sat down next to him for breakfast and told him I hadn't known that a massage could take away that much pain.

"Me, neither," he said.

"You have strong hands," I said. "Warm hands, too, and you really know how to use them. I feel good today still."

"I'm glad you're feeling better, Gina," he said.

"Christopher, do you want to go to church with me next Sunday?"

"That's a good idea. I haven't been to church in a long time. I used to go with my mom when I was growing up. Every Sunday. We never missed."

The next Sunday we went to church together and I went up to light a candle for my grandmother. I said a prayer for her and I prayed about my past too and thanked God for letting me meet Christopher.

After seeing Ruben again, I had been having bad dreams about returning to the life I had led. I prayed I wouldn't do that, and I asked God to let me forget drugs.

I went back to the pew and realized how good it felt to have Christopher sitting next to me in church. I hadn't been to church since I was a little girl with my daddy, but I felt that God watched over me. Every time I had gone through a hardship, every time I had almost lost my life, he brought me back. I knew it was him doing that.

I just didn't know why.

My mother had always told me that whenever something bad happened to me, God was ready to bury me. She told me that over and over.

I realized, sitting there next to Christopher, that wasn't true.

Christopher and I had gotten closer even though I still hadn't told him anything about my past. I thought he was a man I could count on.

After the first night when we were intimate in the tub, though, when I wanted to be intimate with him again, he wouldn't come near me. He was affectionate to me otherwise, but he wouldn't come near me again for a while.

The next time he came back from Europe, we were in bed together and he got me very excited as he lay on top of me, but after five minutes, he just rolled off.

He had been touching me and kissing me and caressing my privates, but when the time came to make love, he got off. I thought maybe he'd get back on in a second to finish making love to me.

Instead he just fell asleep.

I felt cold.

I couldn't go to sleep for a while and I put my hands on his stomach. Then I gently scratched his back. He snored.

He slept through to the morning.

He got up around five thirty to go to work. He didn't kiss me. He just got up and took his shower.

I pretended to sleep.

Usually he would come and kiss me before he left, but he didn't that morning. I heard the front door shut and then he was gone.

When it came to sex, he was different.

I was frustrated.

When he came home that night, he brought me flowers and told me he was going to take me out to dinner. He apologized for not calling me from his office that day. He had been busy, he said.

Usually he called me all the time.

That night I tried again to make love to him, but he did the same thing.

He wouldn't … or couldn't … satisfy me.

Maybe it was because I was twenty-four and he was thirty-seven, I thought, but I was afraid to talk to him about it because I thought he would be too embarrassed.

This went on for months.

One day I was talking to my mom and I told her that Christopher was so good to me, but he was different from other men. He wasn't cold. He was affectionate, but I told her what happened when we were about to have sex.

She told me some men were like that. She told me she went out with one man for a long time and he was like that. He was so nice, though, that she didn't have the guts to get rid of him. Finally she was just too miserable to continue seeing him.

I told her I needed more affection.

She told me to try one more time. Give him another chance.

"But something's wrong," I told her.

"I know exactly what you're going through," she said.

So I gave Christopher another chance because he was such a nice man. He gave me presents. He took me to restaurants. He bought me clothes. He even gave me money.

Christopher told me that his parents were coming to visit him. They hadn't seen him for a long time. He was going to put them up in a hotel because they were only going to stay four days and because their schedules and routines were too different from his to stay at the apartment, he said.

Christopher had told his mother about me in his letters to her and she had replied that she couldn't wait to meet me. She had wanted him to bring me to Europe to visit, but he said he couldn't.

I had decided by then that Christopher just didn't understand about being intimate with women.

I didn't want to hurt Christopher or his parents, though, so I didn't tell him I really didn't think it was a good idea for me to meet his family.

At that time I hadn't seen any of my old friends for a long while because I was trying to stay dried out. I was frightened even of going to restaurants or clubs by myself because of the temptations there.

I realized all I had was Christopher. He had become my drug.

When his mother and father came, I went out to dinner with them.

When his mother first saw me, she seemed in shock and she kept looking at me.

Finally she said, "You're so beautiful."

I guess she was surprised Christopher was with someone like me.

At the restaurant I enjoyed their company. I loved to be with older people, maybe because they reminded me of my grandmother.

After dinner we walked up Madison Avenue. They loved to window shop in New York. His mother was a little surprised as she watched the other women walking by her that at that hour they were not more dressed up, like she was. A lot of the girls were working girls and they wore slacks or even jeans. But she looked quite perfect, her hair and her dress, and she was still a very pretty woman. My grandma would have loved to watch her walk down Fifth Avenue.

I thought she was used to Europe and used to people with money.

We finally walked back to their hotel and I waited downstairs while Christopher escorted them up to their room. His mother gave me a little kiss and a hug before they got on the elevator. So did his father.

When Christopher came back down, I told him he had nice parents.

"They are very nice," he said. "I told you I was adopted, right?"

"You did," I said.

"My real mom wasn't married. She and my father had almost gotten married, but then something happened," he said. "My mom gave me up for adoption at two months and that's when they got me. They sent me to a boy's school in England and then to a good college here. Without them I wouldn't be what I am."

I would no longer try to go near Christopher sexually. I would just hug him and kiss him and then go to my own bed in Christopher's converted office. It was a huge, soft bed and I still felt like I was living like a little queen. Just a lonely queen.

I really didn't understand. I felt like I had a friend, not a boyfriend.

One night he came into me. I had been complaining I was cold.

"I can keep you warm," he said and he came into my room and lay next to me.

He started to touch me and I got excited. I had tried so many times to be intimate with him, but I wasn't sure what to do. I wondered if maybe I just excited him too much.

That night he frustrated me again.

I couldn't take it anymore. I knew that if I didn't leave now, it would hurt him even more when I finally did leave.

I didn't want to embarrass him by trying to talk about any of this, and I decided the best thing to do would be to disappear. That way he could decide for himself what had happened and he could always just blame me. He would never be hurt that way.

After he was soundly asleep, I packed my things and tiptoed out of Christopher's before he woke up the next morning.

Chapter Nine

I went back to Bridgeport and I started hanging around bars so I could pick up guys for sex and make a little money.

It was summertime and I had no place to sleep. I'd go down to the beach and lie on the sand, fold my arms and lay my head on them, close my eyes and go to sleep.

Sometimes I'd sleep under the railroad bridge and sometimes I'd check the doors of parked trucks and when I found one that someone had forgotten to lock, I'd crawl onto the seat and sleep there.

I soon was so heavily into drugs then that not even my old friends wanted to know me.

At that time my grandma was very sick. I couldn't help her so I didn't go visit her.

If I called my mom, she would hang up on me as soon as she heard my voice. She had gone home one night and found the mattresses all turned upside down and her drawers all emptied out. The place had been torn apart even though the house had been locked.

I was the only other person with a key so she thought I had done it, but I hadn't. I would never have done that.

All her money and all her jewels had been stolen.

I told her I hadn't done it, but after that she would have nothing to do with me. Neither would my aunt or anybody else.

One night just after that I had fallen asleep in someone's truck, but I woke up starving. I hadn't eaten for a few days.

There was a carnival in Bridgeport then and I snuck in under the back fence and saw a little girl standing next to a game booth with a bag of potato chips. When her mother wasn't looking, I grabbed her potato chips and ran.

I hid behind a corner of one of the booths and ate all her chips. I was starved.

Crouching there, I suddenly wondered if I could have been so stoned that I didn't remember stealing my mother's jewelry.

A couple days later I was hanging around on Main Street in Bridgeport. I was sitting on the curb, my feet in the street, and watching people walk by. Suddenly I saw my mom driving by.

I thought she was going to stop and talk to me, but she just drove on by acting like she didn't know me. I knew she had seen me because she had looked right into my eyes.

I was dirty. I was hungry. My hair was all over the place. I hadn't changed my clothes in I don't know how long. I didn't look good at all. I smelled.

After I saw her drive by, I got up and started walking. My eyes burned because I was crying so hard.

I walked the streets for hours.

Finally I walked into a Stop and Shop and started over to the vegetable department to steal some cucumbers. I could easily slide them right up my sleeve.

A man walked right in front of me and then stopped and stared at me.

"Is that you, Gina?" he asked.

I asked him who he was.

"I'm Jason."

"Oh, Jason!" I said. "I'm glad to see you."

He and I had hung around doing drugs when I was sixteen.

"What are you doing here?" he asked.

"Nothing. I'm just waiting for my mom, but I don't think she's going to show up, sad to say. What are you doing?"

"Nothing. I just wanted to pick up a few things at the store. Then I'm going home. Do you want to come with me?"

I went with him around the store and watched what he was buying. He asked me if I needed anything.

"No. You go ahead," I said.

"I may just want to get some sandwiches," he said. "I haven't eaten yet. Would you like one?"

"I might have one," I said.

I was worried that he was going to make me pay for it, but I figured if I promised him sex after, I'd be okay.

We kept walking around the store and he put other things in his basket. We walked up to the front register and I just followed behind him.

He paid for my sandwich.

We walked outside and he asked me if I wanted something to drink too. We went back inside and I picked out a soda. I couldn't wait to drink it, I was so thirsty. He paid again and we went back outside.

"Come with me," he said.

We walked over to his car and got in it. He didn't look good, I noticed. He was so skinny he looked malnourished. Of course, I didn't look so hot either.

"So, what have you been doing?" he asked. "We haven't seen each other for I don't know how long."

"We haven't, have we," I said.

"I don't live far from here."

I drove home with him and when we got there, we sat down in his kitchen and ate our sandwiches and drank our soda.

"I'm going to make some popcorn," he said. "Want some?"

I said yes. I had eaten all my sandwich, but I was still starving.

I realized I'd known Jason for a long time and so decided I didn't have to be shy with him.

"You know, I have no place to go."

He looked at me, surprised.

"Where's your mom?" he asked. "I thought you said you were waiting for your mom."

"I just said that. She won't talk to me any more. Do you have any eggs? I'd love to cook some eggs because I'm still starving."

"Go ahead. There's eggs and bread all kinds of stuff in the refrigerator."

I helped myself. I cooked some eggs and I made myself some chocolate milk. I loved chocolate milk. The sugar made me feel good.

After I had finished eating, I was sitting there at the table when suddenly the tears started dripping down my cheeks.

This man was helping me.

I had been living in the street for several weeks. I hadn't eaten well for days. I had only five quarters in my pocket. I looked dirty. I smelled.

But he was helping me.

"After you've eaten," he said, "I'll tell you some things and you can tell me some things, okay?"

"Jason, if you hadn't picked me up, I would probably have starved to death in the street."

"How long have you been in the street?" he asked.

"A week or so. This time."

"You haven't eaten all this time?"

"Yes, I did, but I haven't eaten in the last few days. I'm out of money."

He told me to take all my clothes off. I thought he was ready to jump into bed with me, but he walked out of the room. I wondered if he wouldn't come near me because I smelled so bad.

He went into his dresser drawer and got me a tee shirt and a pair of shorts.

I changed into them and he threw all my old clothes into the garbage.

"What are you doing today?" I asked him.

"I've got to go out and get a few things," he said.

"Do you mind if I stay here. I really need to sleep."

I went and looked in his bathroom mirror. My eyes were dark. My hair was scattered all over the place and I was very dirty. I hadn't washed my face or brushed my teeth in I don't know how long. I asked him if he had an extra toothbrush.

"I've got a lot of them. They're not opened. They're in the cabinet there. Help yourself."

I brushed my teeth and took a long bath and then rinsed off in a shower.

"Boy, you smell good," Jason said to me. "What'd you use?"

"Soap and shampoo."

I made some coffee in his kitchen and I put a lot of sugar and a whole bunch of milk in my cup.

He looked at my cup and asked me why I just didn't drink milk.

"I only like milk in coffee," I said. "That way it's warm. Can I use your phone?"

He said sure and I went into the living room and dialed my mother. Her answering machine came on, as I knew it would, and I just let her know I was okay.

I went back into the kitchen.

I sat down next to him at the table and he said, "So tell me about yourself. What have you been doing?"

"Drugs," is all I said.

He was quiet for a moment and then he asked me "What size are your jeans? We're going to go to the store and get you a couple pair of jeans and a couple shirts."

I went with him and got some jeans, some shorts and some tee shirts. He gave me fifty dollars in cash too.

I told him I'd pay him back.

He told me I could stay with him until I got myself straightened out. I had no other place to go, he said.

After we finished shopping, he told me he had to go to New York to deliver something to a friend of his. He invited me to go with him and I decided I'd go. I really wanted to sleep, but he was being so nice to me, I felt I should keep him company.

I knew he was either delivering drugs or delivering money to buy drugs with, but I didn't ask any questions. I just went along.

That night we came back and drove all the way to New Haven to deliver something else. I still didn't ask any questions. We got home really late.

When we got back into his kitchen, he showed me a little packet and asked me if I had ever taken it.

"What is it?" I asked.

"It's Cannabinol," he said. "It's very strong. You only take a little bit of it."

I took a little pinch and snorted it.

"Wow," was all I could say.

Almost immediately I lost any sense of myself. I had no idea where I was.

I don't remember anything else that happened.

The next day Jason told me I had gone crazy.

I had taken all my clothes off and went running outside and then started screaming as I ran down the sidewalk. He had to chase me down and tackle me in order to bring me back inside. After that he locked the door and wouldn't let me leave.

"You shouldn't take any more of that," he said. "It's too strong for you. You went nuts."

That day we drove to New Haven and brought a package to a motorcycle club there. We drove around to quite a few other places and didn't get back home until the next morning. I was exhausted.

We slept a little but when I got up, I still felt very tired. Some of that, though, was the Cannibinol. It had really knocked me out. I told Jason I wanted to stay home for the rest of the day. I felt worn down. I could hardly stand up and my eyes were so, so tired. He said okay.

I felt a little nauseous, too, but after he left I made myself some eggs and toast. I kept eating and eating. I must have eaten five pieces of toast and three eggs and I was still starved after that. Jason had a lot of junk food in his cabinets and I went after that like I'd never eaten before.

After a couple months living like that with him, I had gotten fat.

I couldn't stand myself.

I told Jason that I thought I was getting fat and he told me, "Yes, you are. Maybe you sleep too much. All you're doing is eating and sleeping. A walk would do you good."

I started getting up early in the morning and jogging. I started taking a lot of vitamins and supplements. I'd walk during the day. I stopped eating his junk food.

After two or three weeks of my new routine, I was getting better. I told him I appreciated all he'd done for me and told him that without him, I'd still be in the streets.

Then one day he went out early in the morning and didn't come back home. For some reason, some sixth sense, I knew something had happened to him.

When I finally heard him drive up, I opened the door and thought at first I was seeing things. His face was all bloody and had been slashed by a knife or maybe a razor.

"What happened to you?" I asked. "Your face is all sliced up. It's bad."

"This girl and I got into a fight," he said. "She got mad at me. I don't even know what I did. She took out a razor and just started slicing my face. Maybe she was taking too much of that drug. Who knows?"

I told him he needed to go to the hospital. He needed stitches.

"You're a handsome man," I said, "and if you don't go get stitches, you'll have a face full of ugly scars." He had to get stitches, I told him.

I gave him a towel and told him to hold it up against his face to stop the bleeding a little. I helped him out to his car and drove him to the emergency room.

He got thirty stitches in his face and I cried the whole time. I felt so sorry for him. He had been a handsome man, but I worried that he'd still need surgery afterward.

He didn't go out for a while after that, but I was afraid that girl would come around and get mad at me if she found me there.

I told Jason that I thought I ought to leave. I didn't know what his girlfriend might do. I could go to Florida because I still had friends down there, I said, but he wouldn't let me go.

A week later I decided I'd get a job. I had lost the weight I'd gained, I felt like I was recuperating and I was feeling pretty good. But I still had no money in my pocket. Nothing.

I went to a bar in New Haven that I used to go to and asked the manager for a job. He gave me a job waitressing.

There was another girl working there and when I told her I was looking for a place to stay, she said I could share her apartment with her. Her roommate had moved out and gone back home.

I moved in, but didn't stay there long.

I just made enough money so I could get to Florida. Key West. My father had lived there and even after he died, I had gone back there a few times because I had a cousin who lived there.

I moved in with her again until I ran out of the money I had made in New Haven. She worked every day at a local fish farm and she always smelled like fish. I finally told her I was going to Miami to look for a job there.

I never knew what was going to happen to me when I went out into the world. I never really knew where I was going. I never had a plan. Somehow, I liked it that way. It was like I was putting myself in God's hands.

People always feel, when something bad happens to them, that God is testing them, like he tested Job. What's funny is that when people do something they know is bad, they're testing God.

And that's a sin.

Chapter Ten

I had my backpack with me and I started walking and hitchhiking to Miami. I actually hoped somebody would pick me up who I could go home with.

No one would pick me up all day.

It started to get dark. I saw a factory on the other side of a parking lot and there were a lot of folded cardboard boxes in the back piled high on pallets.

I went around to the boxes and pulled one off and opened it up. It was huge and long, just like a coffin. I lay it down and crawled inside to sleep.

It was getting chilly, so I put on all the clothes I had. My extra socks, a sweater. I still was cold and shaking a little bit, but I was mostly tired from all the walking I'd done. I was a little scared too.

Before I closed my eyes, I prayed.

The next thing I knew it was light outside.

I took my pack and started walking again. I wanted to eat, but I didn't have much money with me, just some loose change in the bottom of my pocket.

After I had walked for a while, my feet started to hurt and I sat down on the side of the road.

I started thinking that some kind of bad man would pick me up and rape me and then just throw my body somewhere in the woods. I said to myself today might be the last day I was going to stay on this earth.

I knew it was dangerous to be by myself out there. I started praying while I walked.

I walked and walked until I was so tired I couldn't walk anymore. The sun was about to set. It was beautiful going down, yellow and a little red, and I just sat there and watched it. I lay down away from the side of the highway on a large stone slab I found. No one could see me. It was still warm from the day's sun and I closed my eyes and fell asleep on it.

I dozed for a few minutes, but it was still light so I walked back over to the highway and started to hitch hike again.

A husband and wife stopped and picked me up.

They asked me where I wanted to go and I asked them where they were going. They were driving to Pompano Beach. I said I was going to Miami, but they could drop me off wherever they were going.

I got into the back seat of their car and just sat there silently as they drove along. I didn't ask any questions or say anything.

Finally they said they wanted to stop and get something to eat because they were starving. They'd been on the road for a while.

We stopped at a nice restaurant and as they went in, I told them I was just going to walk around a bit. I wasn't going inside. They asked if I was sure and I said yes.

I couldn't afford to go into the restaurant, of course, but not too far away I saw a MacDonald's. I walked in and got myself a bag of French fries for a dollar.

They had left their car unlocked for me so I went back to it and sat in the back seat waiting for them. When the woman got back in the front seat, she was carrying a bag in her hands.

"I brought you the rest of my sandwich," she said, "because they gave me way too much food. I couldn't eat it all. I've got a Coke too. Do you want it?"

I was starving. The bag of French fries did nothing to fill me up.

She handed over the rest of her club sandwich, some French fries and a Coke that was still almost full. I asked her if she might not want to save it so she could drink it later. She said no, if I wanted it, I could have it.

I ate everything and I drank the Coke too.

I thanked her so much.

I asked if they minded if I lay down a little bit and they said no, help myself. I lay on the seat, closed my eyes and slept like a baby until I felt the car stopping.

The woman turned around in her seat and said, "I don't think it's safe for you to hitch hike. Especially a pretty girl like you. My husband and I will take you to the bus station and you can take a bus to Miami."

I told her I didn't have any money. She said they would take me to the bus station and they'd buy me a ticket.

I told her, no, I'd be fine. I could hitch hike.

"No. We're taking you to the bus station," she said.

When we got to the station, the lady told me, "You're so pretty. I'd feel better that you take a bus so you'll be safe." She bought me a ticket and gave me thirty dollars cash so I could get something to eat.

"You've got a long way to go, you know," she said.

I couldn't believe how nice they were. I asked if I could have their address so I could mail them their money back when I got it. She said no, she just had wanted me to be safe.

"You take care of yourself," she said.

"Thank you," was all I could say.

When I got to Miami, I got off the bus and went to find a phone to call my old friend Joe. He had told me that if I ever came to Miami, I should look him up.

I had kept his phone number all this time. He'd been the boy I gave grass to the day my daddy died.

I kept calling and calling. It was getting very late. I dialed his phone the fifth time and he picked up.

"Joe," I said to him. "This is Gina."

"Gina! Where are you?"

"I'm at the Miami bus station."

"It's a little far from where I live, but I'll pick you up. Don't move. Stay right there. It'll take me about thirty minutes to get there."

I felt blessed.

I waited for him at the bus station under a big clock on the wall so I could keep track of the time. He had said thirty minutes, but after an hour he hadn't arrived. Maybe I wasn't so blessed.

I thought I'd have to sleep in the street or behind some building.

A man walked in front of me looking around and looking around. He had long hair and was very skinny. I didn't think it was Joe. He had always had short hair. He wouldn't have long hair like that, I thought. This man's hair was half-way down his back. I stood up anyway so he could see me, in case it was Joe.

"Hey!" he yelled and threw his hands up in the air. "Hey, Gina!"

"Is that you, Joe?" I yelled.

"Yeah! What's the matter?" He walked over to me.

"I didn't know you had long hair. I didn't recognize you."

"It's me, all right. C'mon. Let's go."

He gave me a hug as we walked out of the bus station.

"Joe, how are you doing?" I asked him.

"I'm doing fine. I'm okay. How about you?"

"You know me. I'm falling apart here and there."

"Well, you look great. What's happened?"

"A lot has happened," I said. "I don't even know where to start to tell you."

"Was it bad or good?"

"Some's been okay. Some's pretty bad. We'll sit down and I'll tell you about it. You look good. Only your hair is kind of long."

"It's a kick," he said. "I don't have to get a hair cut any more. I hated getting haircuts. And the money I save! Just kidding. You must be hungry after your trip, huh? I'm a little hungry myself. I've been off fishing with my friend all day. I fish a lot. That's my hobby."

"Wow. I like to fish," I told him.

"You'll have to come with me then. It was hot today, but it was nice out on the ocean."

I realized just how dark he was from the sun. Dark skin and long hair. That's why I hadn't recognized him.

We were driving along and I recognized a restaurant I had gone to once. I pointed it out to Joe and to my surprise he pulled in.

"Joe, this is too nice a restaurant. I don't look good."

"People wear all kinds of things these days. You always look good. You're about the most beautiful girl I've ever known, Gina. Don't you know that? Let's go in."

"Okay," I said.

After I sat down inside, I started to worry. I knew I couldn't pay to eat. I only had the thirty dollars the lady had given me and I wanted to keep it, just in case.

Joe was staring at me from across the table. "So what brings you here?"

"It's a long story, Joe. I hitch hiked most of the way here," I said.

"That's a dangerous thing to do. You're just looking for trouble."

I didn't feel scolded. I felt he cared, and I just wanted to open up to him. It felt safe.

"You know, Joe. I want to tell you something. I really don't even know why I'm still alive. After my father died, I wanted to kill myself and I bought three bags of cocaine and heroin. I had my friend take me to an empty warehouse and sit there with me until I had done it all. I didn't think he would stop me. Finally he told me he was going home. I'd be all right, I said. I was just going to sleep there that night. I knew I had no place to go, no place to stay, no friends, no one. I told him to just leave me there. I didn't want to live anymore. I was tired of running around and doing whatever it was I was doing. I was down because of my dad. You remember my dad, right? He threw you out that day and then was electrocuted at work. It was my fault. Do you remember how upset he was when he threw you out?"

"Oh, yeah, I remember. I never wanted to bother him again so I never went back there to see you after that. I'm sorry. And I never called you."

"That night in the warehouse," I said, "my friend did leave me there. The next thing I knew, I opened my eyes and I was in a hospital. My friend had finally decided to come back for me. I asked him why. He told me he wasn't sure, but when he got back there, he saw I had turned blue and that's when he went and called the ambulance. I didn't look too good, he said."

Joe was just looking at me.

"I don't do that stuff anymore," Joe said. "I don't even drink anymore. I finally slowed down because so many of my friends died of overdoses. They might as well have just killed themselves. That wasn't even real life, Gina. I told myself one day that I had to quit. If you want to quit drinking and taking drugs, you have to do it yourself. No one can do that for you. You have to want to quit."

"Yeah. With me, every time I go to rehab, I always go back to the same pattern, over and over. I just don't learn my lesson. Maybe I'm just too weak. I don't know."

"You're young," Joe told me. "You could turn your life around. You can't "fly" every day. You don't have any wings, do you? Don't fly anymore, Gina. I know when you take drugs, you think you're flying. You feel good. But that's not real life. I don't think I'll ever go back to the way I was in the past. It's a new me now. The old Joe is gone. I told him good bye."

"You're very brave, Joe," I said to him.

Joe's house was in a beautiful, wealthy neighborhood.

All the houses had large yards and sat far from each other. Each one had a large pool. Joe's house was beautifully landscaped with flowers and shrubbery all long the edges of his enormous yard.

"Joe, did you win the lottery?" I asked him.

"No."

"Where'd you get all the money? This house is worth millions of dollars."

"You know what I used to do."

"No, I don't."

He told me he had worked with drug smugglers from the Caribbean and he had saved most of the money he had made.

He was a smart man. He had quit. He didn't even drink anymore. He had quit everything.

"I can't go anywhere anymore though. There's still a fifty-fifty chance someone wants to take my life away. I made so much money then, but I didn't want to hurt others with drugs anymore. My background wasn't like that. My parents came to this country from Italy and they saved every penny they made. They worked hard. My mother worked cleaning hotel rooms her whole life. Hard, hard work. One day I finally said to myself, "What am I doing?" I told myself that this wasn't life, the way I was living, the things I was doing. You remember what we used to do. Selling drugs. You and I even got caught once and went to jail for a little while, remember?"

"Yes, I remember," I said.

"Now I work disciplining other bad kids. They've been on drugs. They've been abused by their parents. Some don't even have any parents. When I was little, my parents could not control me. I went out there, very young, and I did what I did. Because I was such a bad kid growing up, I know exactly how to handle the kids I work with."

"Joe," I said, "If any kid even looks at you, you're so big and so strong, he's just going to sit down and obey you. He'll be afraid of you just because you're so big."

He started laughing.

"You did the right thing, Joe," I told him. "I'm happy for you. Do you date?"

"Yes, I date. I'm supposed to get married, but we haven't decided when."

"Where is she?" I asked.

"She's still in college. She'll graduate next year. When she comes home, she comes here."

"Wow. You turned your life around. The last time I saw you, you were a drug addict. Now you're in heaven."

"You're right. I'm happy. I help people and I make others happy. Those kids are like my kids. I adore them. I'm with them all day. Now I'm teaching another person there to do what I do."

"That's wonderful," I said.

"Yeah."

I asked Joe if I could go and get cleaned up. I hadn't had a shower for several days. Joe told me to make myself at home.

After I had taken my shower and cleaned up, Joe showed me the kitchen and asked me if I wanted something to eat or drink. "Help yourself," he told me.

I opened the refrigerator. It was the size of one in a restaurant. You could see all the food lined up behind the glass panels. He had it all so organized, meat with meat, drinks with drinks, vegetables with vegetables, all separate.

"Oh, my God," I said. "Joe, can I have some fruit?"

"I told you, don't ask. Just help yourself. Make yourself at home. Enjoy it. I have guests here all the time. Sometimes I have people down from Connecticut and they stay for a month or two. When my parents come, they just walk in and walk out. This house is open. I don't even lock the door. I have a lot of company, especially in the winter, when my friends come south from the cold."

I was standing there in his kitchen still wet from the shower. He looked at me right in the eye when he'd finished talking.

"Gina," he said. "You are so beautiful! Too bad we split up because of your father."

"Yeah. I went back to Connecticut then. You're all set, Joe, but my head is still spinning. I'm never settled. I'm happy you're successful. You're so thin, though. What are you doing with that? You don't eat or what?"

"You know why I'm thin? Every morning I take the kids running non-stop for an hour. We're very busy. I teach them sports. We go fishing. I'm not mean to them, but I do discipline them. It takes a while to calm them down, but sooner or later they recognize who they are and they start behaving."

"Joe, you're so different. You even look different."

"When you get older, things change. Sometimes they change for the worse. Sometimes they change for the better. You can change too. I know that drugs have got you. I know. I've had quite a few friends die from drugs. Others are still in jail. You've known some of them. Some of them took so many drugs that their brains are done. You can't talk to them. You can't do anything with them. They just sit in their chairs. Some moan. I decided I didn't want to be that way. I didn't want to disappoint my parents, either, because they had worked so hard for me. I respect them now. I know they love me. They would have done anything to make a better life for me. Especially my dad. Now I can show them how good I really am."

We went into the living room and sat down on a beautiful black leather sofa. He told me he had only been living there for about eighteen months. He had done all the outside landscaping himself.

I told him it was beautiful.

"I've always kept you in my mind, Joe. You remember, before we went to jail, we were hanging around with all of those guys. No one had any money. No one had a job. They talked about robbing a bank, but that was before you and I had ever been to jail together. Then, after we had gotten out of jail, you were hanging around and these guys and they were still practicing how they were going to rob a bank. There were six of you, right? You all had guns. You had the rifle?"

"Yeah, I did. I practiced driving the getaway car. That night, when we drove up to the bank, a policeman came up to our car and shined his light in. Two of my friends got scared and shot at the cop. He shot back. All three of them died instantly. More cops swarmed the car, but I threw my gun down on the floor and threw my hands in the air. So did the other three. We didn't shoot anybody, but we went to jail for more than a year. I think someone had overheard us planning to rob the bank and reported us, but I don't know who. If we had done it more quietly, I think we would have succeeded, but we couldn't think clearly then because we were so young and so stoned. It was horrible. My two friends died. I still feel badly about it."

"Joe, I'm exhausted. I should go to bed now. I'm tired of everything. Sometimes my whole body just aches, but I can't go to sleep. Tonight I think I'll go to sleep. Thank you for bringing me here."

That night he came into my room and said to me, "You know, I always liked you. We've known each other for how long now?"

"A while, Joe"

"I felt bad about your father and I was sad when you left. I've always thought about you, too. A lot. I'd say to myself that I hoped you were doing well. I'm glad you came."

He gave me a big hug and kissed me on the forehead. "Sleep well. You know what? I get up very early, at six in the morning, but you stay in bed as long as you want. You look tired. You know where everything is, the refrigerator and all that. Can you cook?"

"Yes, I can."

"I don't know what time I'll be home, but maybe you can call me later. I'll leave my phone number in the middle of the kitchen table. If anything is wrong, call me. I'll be back later. We'll go out to eat. There's a lot of nice restaurants right around here."

"Thank you again, Joe. I know I keep saying it, but I'm very happy for you."

After he left my bedroom, I began to feel that everyone was doing well except me. I was still doing the same things and not changing. I looked at the way Joe looked and I looked at myself. My head kind of popped.

I began to think of my guardian angel.

Chapter Eleven

The next morning I could see the sun shining through my window. It was still early, but I got up. I looked outside. It was beautiful. You could see the houses far away across the neighborhood.

I went into the kitchen just as Joe was coming downstairs. I told him I wanted to make him his coffee and breakfast, if he wanted it.

"Coffee's fine," he said. "Do you know where it is?"

"Yep. It's right here." I opened the cabinet.

"I go to work early so I'm there when the kids get up. Then I eat breakfast with them."

I poured him a cup of coffee when it was ready and he took it with him. He kissed me on the forehead again on his way out, gave me a little hug and told me to have a nice day.

After he left, I went back to bed. I just lay there for a while, still thinking of my guardian angel. He was in real estate then. He bought houses, renovated them and sold them. I knew that if I ever went to live with him, he would give me a nice home.

I kept thinking about him. For all these years I had always gotten help from him if I was in big trouble. He'd said the door was always open for me.

It suddenly dawned on me. My guardian angel was in love with me.

I thought about how Joe was living now and I thought maybe I could live like that too. I got up and went out to the phone and dialed my guardian angel's number. I knew it by heart.

"Where are you," he asked me immediately. "Are you all right?"

"Yes. I'm in Florida."

"You're in Florida? I haven't heard from you. I thought you were with your mom again because you hadn't called. Are you going to live in Florida now?"

"No. I've been in Key West with my cousins, but I got a little bored so I came to see a friend of mine. He's got a beautiful home here in Miami. I met him when I had lived in Florida. He's a nice man."

"If you want me to come and pick you up at the airport, just tell me what day, what plane, what time. I'll come pick you up."

I wish you were here," I told him.

"Yeah? I'd like to come to Florida. I'd love to, but I have to finish this house because I've got someone interested in buying it. I'm just about done."

"I'll call you again," I said.

"You take care of yourself," he said. "I'm glad you called. I don't have to worry about where you are now."

"I'm fine here," I said.

I could tell by his voice that he was happy to hear from me. I hung up and went back to bed. I knew he really cared about me.

A few days later I called him back. If I was going home, I had no place to go, I told him. My mom wouldn't talk to me. No one was talking to me. I was all alone. I asked him if I could come stay with him for a few days. I said he was the only one who would talk to me.

He said he'd be happy if I would stay with him.

"I can't wait for you to come back," he said, "and maybe you can help me do things with this house. There's lots to do here. I know I need a hand. Just call me when you're coming and I'll pick you up at the airport."

I was happy too. I wouldn't end up back on the streets.

I felt there must have been some reason that I had come to visit Joe. Maybe God was trying to wake me up. I started thinking that I was going to turn around and finally straighten myself out.

If I ever stopped drinking and taking drugs and doing all the other things I had been doing, I could start to think about a future. That had never occurred to me before. When I looked at Joe and saw what he'd done for himself after everything he had been doing, I saw that he had turned his life around. He'd moved from evil to good.

I felt I could do that too.

It was the first time I felt that I could do something for myself, my own future. This time I wasn't going to do it for anybody else. I was going to do it for me.

In the past, every time my mom told me to go to rehab or do this or do that, I tried to make her happy. I went to rehab, but I wasn't taking it seriously for myself.

Now I wanted to do something for myself.

That night I told Joe I had called my friend, the one I called my guardian angel.

"Who's that?" he asked.

"I used to work for him at Friendly's when I was younger," I said.

"You've known this guy a long time then?"

"Yes, but we're just friends."

Joe asked me if I wanted him to take me to one of the restaurants around there.

"You'll like it," he told me. "Besides, you need to go out and go to some places and see some different kinds of people.

He was right.

I cleaned up the kitchen and then went into my bedroom and made my bed. I had been puttering around cleaning up Joe's house all day. I was happy doing that.

Joe had liquor in his refrigerator, but I hadn't touched it. If I could do that now, I could do that all the time, I said to myself. I just couldn't let anything disturb the commitment I had made to myself that day.

I asked Joe if he was okay with my staying there another week or so and he told me to stay as long as I wanted.

I needed the rest. I needed to be by myself. Joe got up early in the mornings and went to work and I could be by myself in his big house.

I'd go outside and cut flowers and bring them in and make arrangements for the kitchen and the living room. I'd take roses and put them in my room. Sometimes during the day I would bend my knees down to the floor and pray. I'd say I wanted to change. I didn't want to be as I had been in the past. I wanted to be renewed. I felt that God would give me the courage to do it. All those years I hadn't been able do it myself.

My guardian angel would help me too.

I needed someone encouraging me. I never had had anyone to tell me what was good for me. I felt that now I had somebody.

I had been waiting for this for a long time.

I prayed before I went to sleep every night too.

The next weekend we were just hanging around. Joe had gotten up early and had been working outside. I had gotten up and was making bacon and eggs and banana pancakes.

Just as the eggs were about done, I went outside and told Joe to come in for his breakfast. He was surprised.

"I thought you were just going to make coffee," he said.

"No, I made a big breakfast. Come in and you can go back outside after."

"This smells so good," he said as he came in. "No one's ever cooked breakfast for me before. I always had to do it myself. This is something new."

He went and washed his hands and came back into the kitchen, sat down and started to eat.

"How'd you know I liked banana pancakes?" he asked.

"I didn't know. That's what I eat in the morning if I feel like cooking."

I sat down with him.

"Joe, I really don't know why I came here looking for you. I just took a chance. If I hadn't found you, I would have ended up back in the street. Not that I haven't done that before. Many times."

"Well, thank God you came," he said.

"I always told myself I should call you, but I didn't know why. Then, a week or so ago, I thought I'd come and I just threw some clothes in my backpack and hitch hiked up here."

"And that's the last time you're going to do that," he said. "I've heard that girls who go out hitch hiking by themselves sometimes never get where they're going. Promise me you'll never do that again."

"Okay, I won't," I said. "You've given me such a good example. If I could do the same thing, I would change. I don't want to be dizzy anymore. Before I get too old and can't do anything anymore, I need to change. Otherwise I'll just be useless, don't you think?"

"I do."

"Every time I'm in the dumps, I go and knock on my guardian angel's door. It's always been open for me, but I never realized how much he really cares for me. I only figured that out the other night. I haven't been able to stop thinking about him. At Friendly's he would always tell me I was a nice girl. We became friends, but I would only go see him when I couldn't help myself. I thought he just liked to help me. We never had sex. He never even touched me."

"I think this man is in love with you."

"I called him a couple days ago and asked if I could go stay with him until I straightened myself out. He said I could and that he'd pick me up at the airport."

"You look happy."

"I am. I really appreciate you letting me stay here too. You're helping me."

"Why don't you stay for a couple more weeks? I don't have anybody coming to visit until next month. Stay here. You're looking good now, you know. You've put a little weight on. That's good."

"Yeah. I feel better. Thank you." I got up and went over and hugged and kissed him. "You are my friend."

"You're my friend, too."

I had mixed feelings about Joe because we had been lovers at one time.

"I'm going to back outside and work a little longer," he said when he finished his breakfast. "Afterward maybe you and I can go out for a drive, if you want, or we can go fishing. Would you like that?"

"Sure. It's a beautiful day. There's no clouds in the sky and it's not even that hot. There's a little breeze."

"You don't have to wear a lot of clothes. Just stay in your shorts and you'll be comfortable."

I washed all the dishes and cleaned up the kitchen. I went upstairs and changed his sheets and made his bed. I took all his laundry down to the laundry room. He had a brand new washing machine, just like the ones in the laundromat, and a beautiful drier. I decided to wait for him so he could show me how to run the machines. They seemed complicated to me and I didn't want anything to happen to his laundry.

I called out to him and asked him to come in and show me how to run his washer.

"I need help. I'm doing your laundry," I told him.

"You are?"

He came and showed me how. It was easy.

I went upstairs and took a shower. I was waiting for my clothes to wash and dry, too, and I was standing there in my bathrobe when I heard Joe come in the house. I peeked out into the hall and saw all he had on was his shorts. He'd been working in the yard and he was hot and sweaty.

I heard him go in and take a shower and then I heard him call out, "Gina, where are you?"

"I'm in my room."

"Why are you staying in there?" he asked.

"I'm waiting for my clothes to dry."

"What? You have no extra clothes?"

"No."

"Well, you could have gone shopping, you know."

"I didn't want to drive your car when you weren't around." He had a brand new Thunderbird in the garage. I couldn't wait to sit in it, but I wasn't going to drive it. He had told me we weren't going to take his truck that afternoon, but his new convertible instead.

"I saw your new car, Joe. I even walked over to it and touched it. It's beautiful."

Joe came in my room and came up close to me. I looked at him and he looked right back. He touched my hair.

"What beautiful hair you have. So thick. And so curly. That's the style now, isn't it? Any girl would want her hair like yours.

I kissed him on the cheek and slid my arms under his. He kissed me and held me very tightly.

"Joe, maybe this would be the wrong thing," I said.

Neither of us said anything else and as our bodies came together, my feelings went back to what they'd been for him earlier. I was lonely. I hadn't had anybody show me any affection for a long time.

I hugged him. He was so warm.

I kissed him. He kissed me again.

"I was in love with you," he said, "and I still have those feelings."

We kissed each other again and then we made love.

Afterward I cried on his shoulder.

He wiped my tears away and said, "My baby. Don't cry. From now on I think you'll be fine."

We hugged each other and I didn't say anything. We just lay on the bed together for the next few hours.

"You made me feel good," he said.

"So did you, me," I said. "You know, I still have the same feelings too. I've always thought about you."

"You were only a little kid then," he said.

"I was seventeen," I said.

"C'mon. Let's get going," he said and kissed me on my forehead.

We got up and I went to get our clothes from the drier. Then we went for a long ride.

It was a beautiful day, one I won't forget.

Chapter Twelve

I never made it to my guardian angel's.

Before I left Joe's, I called my cousin in Key West to say goodbye and she told me she had a friend who was driving up to New York the next day. Maybe he could give me a ride.

I thought that would be a great way to surprise my guardian angel. I could just walk up to his door after I took a train or bus from the city.

But it turned out the guy who drove me up to New York was running drugs.

By the time we got to the city, I was shooting up with him every couple hours.

I stayed with him for a while. We'd bring drugs to the city and sell them and then drive back down to Key West for more.

On our fourth trip up we were stopped by the cops as we pulled into Manhattan.

I spent the next three months in jail. When I got out, I had nothing. I had no money. No clothes. Nothing. Not even any drugs.

I went to Greenwich Village because I knew so many places there. I went into one bar and just stood against the wall for a while, and finally a guy I had known before invited me to sit down at his table with some friends.

They said they hadn't seen me for a long time and I told them what had happened to me. They asked me where my friend was and I told them that was a long story.

They bought me drinks. They were eating and I was starving because I hadn't eaten all that day. I ordered a double cheeseburger with French fries. I was nervous because I thought I might have to pay for my meal and I had no money.

We sat there for a long time and talked. I was wearing high heels and my dress was short. I knew my legs looked nice.

I hoped some man there would start paying attention to me.

Since I had been twelve or so, I had always gotten a lot of attention. I was the only girl in the house and even my father would pay a lot of attention to me.

Whenever I went out, everyone looked at me.

I got a lot of attention.

When my parents' relationship started to break down, I felt I no longer got that attention. I started hanging around my grandma or my aunt and I started to isolate myself from my father. I got no more affection, no more love from him. Maybe that's why I went out into the world, looking for affection, looking for love.

I was suddenly alone.

My father had always come in to my room and kissed me before I went to sleep. He'd read me stories. He'd hug me. He'd tell me he loved me. He'd give me my baths and blow dry my hair. He'd tell me how beautiful I was and say that I was his princess.

He'd always say, "I love you, sweetheart."

When he left, I started making new friends and I went into the streets with them. I didn't know I was going to run into any problems. Nobody was giving me any direction. Nobody told me what I was doing was not right for me.

Nobody warned me.

I started smoking when I was nine. I'd steal my aunt's cigarettes and go outside and smoke with the other kids in her neighborhood. We thought we were making ourselves like older people. All of us smoked and drank then too.

I was nine when I had my first beer. I went to a party with a bunch of older kids and when no one was looking, I took a beer and mixed it in with my Coke so they wouldn't know what I was drinking.

Every night when I went to bed in those days, I thought about my father. I just wished he was there to hug me and give me a kiss and tell me he loved me.

It took me along time to get used to him not being there telling me he loved me.

I would ask my grandma why he left me. I didn't understand. I was little. At first I thought he'd come back home, and I waited for him to come back home for a long time.

Life was painful.

When I hung around with the kids in the streets, we'd drink and smoke grass.

After my dad died, I tried to forget him. I knew he'd never come back into my arms again or tell me he loved me. He'd never tell me I was his princess again.

I had to get my love from someplace else then. Drugs and booze were just like love.

My friends paid for my cheeseburger when they left, and I sat all alone at the table.

An older man who had been drinking at the bar since I came in, beckoned me over to him with his finger.

I went home with him and stayed with him for a few days.

He gave me money, but no drugs.

I decided to go back to Trumbull and get some of the clothes I had left at my mother's house. I was just going to sneak in when she wasn't there and take them. I knew my brother had had to go into an institution, so I figured my mother might be working during the day.

I called a friend to drive me to my mother's. When we got there, her car was in the driveway. I decided maybe I would talk to her.

I went up and rang the bell, but there was no answer. I continued to ring the bell, and I thought maybe she had gone to a neighbor's house.

I kept ringing the bell. Finally I told my friend we should just break in. We walked around to the back of the house to try to force the back door open. One of the back windows was open a little, though, and I opened it and climbed in. My friend waited outside.

I thought no one was home so I went into my room and started rummaging through the closet for some of my clothes.

Suddenly I noticed the smell.

It was gas.

I thought I'd better call my grandma and let her know, but when I went into the kitchen for the phone, I saw my mother had turned on the stove and had put her head in the oven. The smell of gas was overwhelming.

My mom had already passed out and was barely breathing.

I turned off the stove and opened all the windows in the kitchen. I dragged my mother outside. I went back in and called the ambulance, even though I thought she was dead.

When the ambulance arrived, one of the paramedic tended to my mom while the other went into the kitchen and looked around.

When he came out, he asked me if I smoked. I said I did.

"You're one lucky girl," he said. He told me that if I had lit a match, I would have blown the house and myself up into the sky.

I got in the back of the ambulance with the other paramedic and my mother and we started to the hospital. He was giving her oxygen. In a few minutes she opened her eyes and the paramedic asked he if she had taken anything.

"I took a bottle of sleeping pills," she said, "and I washed them down with a pint of Vodka."

She looked very sick.

If I hadn't gone there to get my clothes, she'd have been dead.

Something or someone had told me to go there. I knew that. It was a miracle. I decided that maybe because I had wanted to kill myself many times, I just knew.

And maybe God helped me know.

They kept her in the hospital for several weeks.

"What's the use to live?" she would ask me. She had put my brother away in a mental hospital, so she didn't have him. My other brother had left home, gotten married and had moved to Florida. She had given up on me.

She had no one.

She told me she didn't want to live anymore.

I told her she had to keep herself alive because Jimmy, my brother in the institution, still needed her badly and I did too.

I stopped drinking for a while and stayed with her.

But slowly things would start popping into my head again about my dad and I started drinking again and taking drugs to forget everything I had in my mind.

One night after that I drank too much and I went of crazy. I started screaming. I sliced my wrists. I decided I didn't want to live either.

When I woke up, I was weak and there was a puddle of dried blood around me on the floor of my mom's kitchen, but I was still alive.

Life was too hard. I was in pain all the time.

I was just like my mother. I had no one.

I ended up in a mental hospital in Bridgeport. I stayed there for three months in their detox facility. It was difficult. Even though I'd quit liquor and drugs, I still had all the other stuff in my mind.

A friend had heard I was there and came to visit me one day. He and I had been selling drugs together and he thought he'd fallen in love with me.

I told him I was in pain.

The next day he brought me some heroin and I started using again while I was still in the detox program.

Before that, while I was still dried out, I had written my mother and my grandma and my aunt letter after letter. None of them wrote me back.

When I left the hospital that time, I finally did stay with my guardian angel for a while.

He was the only person I had ever met who always understood me, no matter how I was doing. We weren't lovers. We just knew each other and liked each other.

If he kissed me, he'd just kiss me on the cheek.

He never asked me too many questions either. He never told me what I should do. He never said not to do this, not to do that.

He just talked to me, like a friend.

I started working while I was with him. A friend had a nightclub and it was the only place I could find work. I didn't get paid a lot of money, but I made enough to get by.

Then I found out he was selling drugs from his club. He asked me to deliver a few things for him, and I did because I didn't want to get fired. He made a lot of money selling drugs, but I didn't get any of it. I knew he was taking advantage of me.

One night he told me to deliver something and I went. It was pouring rain and so dark I could hardly make out where I was driving.

I was driving very slowly when suddenly I saw a car coming straight at me from across the next intersection. I froze and then felt a sharp pain across the front of my head. The terrible noise of the crash seemed to drown me.

When I opened my eyes, I was in a bed. I knew I wasn't home. I had an intravenous tube in my hand and I couldn't move.

Everything was so blurry I could hardly see.

A nurse asked me if I remembered what happened. I said no, it was pouring rain and this other guy suddenly came right at me. That was all I knew.

The nurse told me I was banged up pretty badly and the car was totaled. I had hit my face and head hard against the steering wheel and the dashboard.

I dozed off and then woke up again. I opened my eyes and still couldn't see well. I thought I was going blind.

I screamed.

A doctor came in and told me I was temporarily blinded because the blow had hit a nerve somewhere in my head. He told me not to worry. It was temporary.

I felt better.

I had broken both my neck and arm and I was told I would be in the hospital until they were healed. My face stayed badly swollen for a long time and it was scratched all over.

Every morning the doctor would come in and ask me how I was doing.

I'd say, "Fine."

"Can you see me?" he'd ask.

"No."

I'd tell him everything was blurry, everything looked kind of white.

He'd tell me I would see again in a few days.

Another week would go by and I still couldn't see.

I started to get scared.

I finally called my aunt and she came to visit me.

Afterward she called my mom and my mom came to see me too. I hadn't seen her for a long, long time.

When she arrived, I could only hear her say hello from the door, but I started crying.

She came over to my bed and held my hand.

I told her that the doctor had been telling me day after day that I would see again, but I still couldn't see. I couldn't even see her.

I could hear her and my aunt crying.

My mom brought in an eye specialist to see me. He examined me and told me not to worry. I'd be fine.

About a week later I finally started to see out of one eye.

A couple weeks after that I was seeing pretty clearly again.

Those nights in the hospital, when I was going to sleep, I'd pray not only that I could see again, but also that God would help me get my life in the right direction and would help me get better.

At least he helped me see, I thought.

My mom and my aunt wanted me to find a place to dry out. I don't know by then how many times I had already been through that. I had promised my mom I would quit drinking and taking drugs, but I'd promised her so many times, she had quit believing me. Now I think she just felt sorry for me in the hospital because I couldn't see.

I went to Fairfield Hills again for detox.

After I had been there for about two months, I started being sick to my stomach all the time. I told my counselor and said maybe I should go home and rest and then come back.

I called my mom and told her I had been throwing up every morning. I couldn't keep my food down. She asked me when the last time I had been to a gynecologist.

I'd never been to one.

She asked me the last time I had sex. I told her it was with my last boyfriend, but I didn't see him anymore.

My mom said I might be pregnant.

I told her if I stayed there, they would make me keep the baby. I'd seen that happen with another girl. I asked my mom if she would take me home.

I couldn't keep a baby, I said. I'm not right, I told her, and I was afraid the baby wasn't going to be right when it was born. I had been drinking too much and taking too many drugs. I didn't want another person to suffer as I had, especially a little child.

In truth I would have loved to have a baby, and I cried and cried when I realized I couldn't have it. Or shouldn't.

I was going to have an abortion. My mom was going to take me and be there with me. I was grateful.

During the abortion I closed my eyes and pretended I was not even in that room. I tried to be someplace else. Then they gave me the anesthesia and I passed out.

After they had finished, it seemed I could remember the sucking sounds.

I was in a lot of pain and I stayed in bed for a few days. It was sad.

I wanted to drink. I wanted drugs.

I left my mom's one night and went and slept behind the restaurant on the corner by the gas station we all used to hang out at as kids.

I woke up early the next morning, got up and hitchhiked to a truck stop in Milford, Connecticut. I walked up to the first trucker I saw going into the restaurant and asked him if he wanted me. I needed money for drugs.

"Come into my truck," he told me. I went with him and climbed up through the door of the tall cab. We crawled back into his sleeper and had sex. I took the money he offered me.

That morning I saw five or six guys. As soon as I had gotten money from the last guy, I went and bought drugs. I was too scared not to take them.

I kept doing that for a few weeks until I had enough money to buy myself some clothes. I bought a new dress and some new shoes.

That night I walked into a bar on Main Street in Bridgeport. I asked the manager if he had a job. I told him I didn't want to be a waitress.

"You look like you'd be good for something," he said. "I have a strip business for stag parties. You could be a stripper. When can you start?"

"Anytime."

"I want you to rehearse," he said and he gave me a video to show me how he wanted me to dance. "Play this and practice and come back in a couple of days. I want to see how you move."

I didn't have a VCR so I called my guardian angel. I told him I needed help. I'd been calling him for a couple weeks and had come by, but he was never home. He told me he had been on a trip to Mexico and he'd just gotten home the night before.

I asked if I could come over and he said yes.

When I got here, I told him I needed to practice dancing for an audition. He put the video on for me and I practiced. He didn't ask any questions. He just sat on his sofa and watched me dance.

I went back to the bar that night and told the manager I was ready. I started dancing.

"You're fine," was all he said.

I kept that job for a month and I made good money. I'd work at night and I'd sleep all day in a little room I had rented in Bridgeport.

The money I made I spent on drugs. I was into cocaine then and used a bit of heroin.

One night I had just finished working and I was by myself. I walked out to my car and suddenly a man came up behind me and hit me on the head so hard I started bleeding.

He forced me into a car and he and some of his friends raped me. I couldn't even tell how many of them there were and I couldn't fight them all off. Finally I just gave in and let them do what they were going to do. I was afraid they would kill me.

When they were done, they opened the door of their car as they drove off and threw me into the street.

I just lay on the street for a while, I don't know how long. I couldn't see straight. There was blood all over my face. I was in pain all over. I wasn't even sure where I was.

Finally I passed out from the pain.

Chapter Thirteen

When I opened my eyes, a doctor was asking me what happened.

The ambulance had brought me to the emergency room. They hadn't found my purse so they had no identification. They hadn't been able to call my family.

The doctor told me I had a long cut down the side of my face.

I told him all that I remembered was that someone had hit me on the head when I went to my car. I told him I had left work about one-thirty. After that I wasn't sure what happened, but I thought someone had taken my clothes off.

Then I remembered that I had drugs in the car.

The doctor told me they had put quite a few stitches in my head. He held a mirror up for me. The side of my face was swollen and was turning black and blue.

The doctor asked me who had done this.

I told him I couldn't see anything. I didn't know.

He told me someone had found me in the street and had called an ambulance, but they didn't know anything about what had happened.

A nurse came in then and said I had no identification, but she wanted to call my parents. I gave her my mother's phone number.

She came back in a little while and told me nobody was home. Nobody had picked up the phone so she left a message. She said she'd keep calling.

I asked the doctor how long I had to stay there and he said they still had to take more x-rays of my head to make sure nothing more serious had happened. He told me I had a very deep cut and he wanted to keep me there for a few days so they could monitor how the stitches were doing.

I fell asleep that night and the next morning when I opened my eyes, the world was blurred. I couldn't see clearly at all. I told the doctor about my vision and told him I was in serious pain and he gave me light prescription drugs for the pain.

The doctor had known I was taking drugs from the blood tests they had done the previous night when I arrived.

The third day I was there the doctor came in and asked me how I was doing. I told him there was still a lot of pain in my head and my face. My vision was still blurry. He told me I'd be fine. My eyes would just take a couple more days to heal.

He said he knew how painful the stitches were for me, but told me I'd feel better when they came out. He was a nice man.

At one o'clock the next morning he came to visit me again. He sat down at the edge of my bed and said, "I know you've been taking all kinds of drugs. Your body has taken quite a toll from them. A pretty girl like you, it's a waste. You should get help."

He asked me how long I'd been doing drugs and I told him for many years. I told him this wasn't the first time I'd ended up in an emergency room either.

"You're so young," he said. "You could do something with your life. We have quite a few girls and boys who come here after taking drugs. Some of them overdose, and those don't make it. You could do something better than that. You're so young."

Five days later I felt much better, but I was still in the hospital.

A policeman came into my room one day to take a statement from me. He asked me if I knew what they looked like and I told him no. I said they had come up from behind me and one grabbed me and hit me over the head. I knew they took off my clothes off and raped me. When I opened my eyes, I was in this room. That was all I knew. The cop was nice, but I was afraid of cops and I didn't want to rat on anybody.

The doctor finally asked me where my family was and I told him there was just my mother. My dad had died.

I was still waiting for my mom to call me. The nurse had kept calling my mom, but nobody answered. I said maybe she was on vacation. I didn't know. I hadn't talked to her for a long time.

The doctor came in to see me again early the next morning. "You've been here for six days now. How are you feeling?"

I shrugged.

"We'll keep you a little longer, I guess," he said.

I told him he was a good doctor. He was young, only in his forties, and he was easy to talk to.

I called one friend and told him where I was. He came to see me and asked what had happened to me. I told him and told him I was in a lot of pain. He told me he'd be back later, and when he returned, he'd brought me some heroin.

I just wanted to stop feeling the pain.

What they gave me in the hospital was not enough.

Now I felt I could finally, really go to sleep and I slept so long time the nurse had to wake me up for dinner the next night.

"You've got to eat," she said, "so you can take your medicine."

I told her I didn't want any medicine. I still had some of the heroin left that my friend had brought me.

"Take this pill," she said. She was mean.

I took it and put it in my mouth, but didn't swallow it. After she left, I went into the bathroom and flushed it down the toilet.

That night I told the doctor this wasn't he first time someone had hit me in the head. It had happened a few times, but never as bad as this time. I told him that my eyes still went a little blurry for a couple minutes. Mostly it was my right eye.

He told me it was because the nerve that went to the eye had been hit so hard.

After he left, I cried for a long time.

I felt sorry for myself. No one had come to see me. My mom still hadn't called me. Neither had my aunt. No one had called me. Only my one friend had come to bring me a little heroin, but he wasn't even a boyfriend.

After another five days I started to feel better and I could see clearly all the time. I asked the doctor when I could leave. He told me he wanted to make sure everything was absolutely okay so I didn't end up back to the hospital.

That night I prayed.

"I think I know that you are with me," I said aloud to God, "and you're always at my side. I've almost been killed so many times, but you always bring me back. I don't know why. There must be some reason you're keeping me alive, but I don't know what it is. I guess I'll have to figure that out for myself. Thank you, though. I've known all along that you were on my side."

The nurse had kept calling my mother and finally, just before I was ready to leave the hospital, she came in and visited me.

She brought my grandma with her. When my grandma first saw me, she started crying. I told her I'd be fine.

"You're going to come home with me," my grandma told me.

The doctor came into my room while my mom was there and he told her I was lucky to survive. I'd been hit pretty badly. I could've gone blind from the blows, he told her, but luckily it turned out only to be temporary.

"How do you feel now?" he asked me.

"I feel good," I said.

"You're going to leave in a couple days," he said, "and you're going to be fine. Get a checkup with your regular doctor every three months, though, for the next year just to make sure there are no blood clots in your head."

"You saved my life," I told him. "Thank you very much."

"I hope I don't see you again," he said.

I told my grandma that one night in the hospital I felt someone holding my hand. I felt warm throughout my whole body and I really wanted to know who it was. At first I thought it was one of the nurses or that doctor himself, but I couldn't see them.

The next day I got up and I felt good. It was as if I could still feel that hand holding mine and it still felt warm. Even my own hand was still warm. I thought it had been a man's hand because the skin was just a little rough.

I told my doctor the next day, but he said it wasn't him. He hadn't been on duty the previous night.

I wondered if it was the hand of God.

Chapter Fourteen

I decided to go back into rehab.

When I entered Newton that time, I saw girls there who were worse off than I. Sometimes I could talk to them, sometimes I couldn't. Some were even be strapped down by the counselors because they were going through such a difficult withdrawal.

When you've been taking drugs and alcohol for so long, your body needs them.

I had been doing them for almost fifteen years by then. I'd think I'd really want to quit, but I'd go right back into them after detox. I was just doing it for my mom or for my grandma, not for me. I just wanted to make them happy and I only made believe I really wanted to quit.

I ended up fooling myself, if not them.

My mom came to think that I was never going to keep my word. For fifteen years I'd been going into detox and coming out and never succeeding. My body needed the drugs.

By now I had been in Newtown three times altogether.

I saw a girl there who was afraid of people. I would watch her every day, and whenever she saw a man, especially, she would look the other way. I had been there for a month and she wouldn't have anything to do with anyone.

When we'd eat or if we went out on a day trip, I'd always try to sit next to her. One day I started to talk to her. She must have gotten used to having me next to her by then because she didn't look away. She must have come to trust me a little bit by then.

I asked her how long she'd been there and she told me she'd been coming in and out of Newtown for a long time. I asked why and she told me she did drugs.

She was a beautiful girl, probably no more than seventeen. She said she'd first come there when she was only fifteen. I knew she was from a different background than I—a rich one—but she still reminded me of myself and when I looked at her, I'd feel sad.

One day she and I went for a supervised walk with a group of the other girls there. We stopped and I sat down next to her. The sun felt nice on our faces after having been inside for so long.

I asked her why she was afraid of people.

She didn't say anything.

I told her I'd never seen her talking to anyone except me, but she didn't want to talk about that.

I asked her how long she'd been taking drugs and she said since she was eleven. I asked who had first given drugs to her, but she wouldn't say anything more.

It had taken her a long time to even open up that much to me.

There was a little library room at Newtown and I asked her one day if she wanted to go there with me and get some books to take back to our rooms to read. She said no. I told her she had to find something interesting to do. She couldn't keep sitting in the corner.

"They'll never let you go home," I said. "You have to show them that you're being yourself again and getting better."

I told her to at least try to talk, even if it was just to say hello to someone. She didn't have to be afraid that someone was going to hurt her there.

I asked her if someone had hurt before.

"My dad," she said.

I told her, "Mine, too."

I told her what my own problems were and why I was there. She looked at me, and I think she wanted to open up.

A few weeks went by and she came to me to talk. She was a quiet girl anyway, but she started to tell me a little about her mother and then she started talking about her father.

She felt as if she no longer had a mother or a father. When she had lived at home, they had a housekeeper who took care of her. Her dad and mom were always out partying. They both drank a lot and they threw parties at home too.

She started drinking liquor when she was nine. She'd take her mom's cigarettes and get something sweet to drink with them. She liked sweet alcohol and she started drinking more and more of it. She became addicted.

She got caught once with liquor in her locker at school and she stopped going to school regularly after that. She found other boys and girls who were drinking then too and they would all bring liquor to school in their soda bottles. Once in class her teacher smelled her breath and told her she smelled liquor.

She should have chewed gum, she told me.

The teacher took her to the principal's office. Her eyes were sleepy from the alcohol and she couldn't concentrate on what she was saying. The principal called her mother and she came and took her home. After that she was caught with liquor time and time again.

Finally her dad took her to a program to try to detox her.

They lived in Greenwich, Connecticut, and her parents were wealthy. She had two brothers, who she had loved to play with when she had been growing up, and she had a grandmother who she loved and who had spent a lot of time with her.

I have a grandmother, too, I told her. She was the one who always made me feel better, I said, and any time I needed help, I would go to her.

That was the way it had been for her, too, but when her grandmother died, she missed her too much to bear. Her life seemed worthless. Her grandmother had been the only one beside their housekeeper who had cared for her, she told me.

When she was little, she even called the housekeeper "mommy." Only as she started to grow up did she realize this woman wasn't her mom. As a little girl, she didn't know. She had always called her "mommy."

The housekeeper had called her "my own little Vanessa."

Vanessa told me that she had never looked her age. She'd always looked older. I told her it was the same with me.

"My body grew up before I did," I said.

From then on she opened up more and more to me.

After Vanessa was released, she went back home and one day, not much later, she called me.

She wanted me to come visit her when I got out. She told me not to worry about clothes. We were about the same size and she had a lot of clothes, shorts and things, which I could wear. It was summer and I didn't have any summer clothes with me, she knew.

She would pick me up at the train station.

I couldn't wait for that day to come.

Vanessa called me back again the next night.

"Gina, It's not the same without you," she said. "I've been home for almost two weeks now and listen to what's happening. My mom won't leave my side now. We went shopping. We went to New York. We visited her friends. We went to restaurants. She's never done that for me before. I think she started to miss me when I was away in rehab. She started to feel sorry for me, I guess. I was so surprised. I get up in the morning and she says, 'Let's go get some exercise!'

and she takes me to her athletic club in Greenwich. I love it. You should see me. I lost weight, even though I'm eating good. I take a lot of vitamins. As soon as I got home, my mom took me for a complete physical. The doctor said I was strong. I'm doing very well. I've had no liquor. My mom doesn't even have it in the house now. Nothing. Here's what's most amazing. My mom's not drinking at all now, not at home, not even out at a restaurant. She must have made up her mind at the same time I did. She used to drink a lot, I told you. But not once since I've been home. She had looked so drained before I went to rehab. Now she looks good. So, everything's good on my part except, Gina, I miss you so much. I'm waiting for you. I'm even cleaning up my room here. I'll move to my brother's room when you come, and you can have my room. Please stay for a couple weeks when you come, okay? I love you."

After we had hung up, I realized how good it was that her mother was working with her. Vanessa sounded so good.

My mother would never do those things for me.

I went back into my room and I cried. I decided I wasn't going to go home after rehab, but I would go visit Vanessa. I'd felt uncomfortable about going to Greenwich before, because my background was so different, but now I wanted to go.

I ended up staying with Vanessa for three weeks and we did a lot together.

We'd go walking up and down Greenwich Avenue. We'd go to the beach. We took a boat across the sound to Long Island.

I told Vanessa I'd never enjoyed myself like that before. I wished life were always that way. What I'd been through in my past, I told her, was hell compared to this.

"I got a job once," I told her, "and I liked it a lot. I was a nurse's aid and I wore a little uniform. I didn't make a lot of money, but I was working. I was happy. I didn't drink then. My mother bought me a car, an old second hand one, but it was mine. One night I met one of my friend's and I said to myself, okay, I'll just snort a little of this heroin, just this one time. Heroin's never a one time thing, though. As soon as it went up my nose, I wanted more. I kept snorting it with my friend and then we shot up for the next three days. I didn't stop until I collapsed. I don't know why I did that. Maybe I'm just weak. I don't know how my mom survived all the hardships I gave her. Finally she just got tired of it. Your mom's different than my mom Vanessa. Of course, you have money and my mom and I don't."

"Let's not think about all that," Vanessa said. "Let's enjoy ourselves."

Vanessa had been about the same age as I had been when she started taking drugs and drinking alcohol. Like me, she didn't know. Vanessa had been in and out of rehab several times, too, but she had never been in jail.

After this rehab, though, she had learned her lesson. She told me she'd never do those things again.

Her father had taken her to quite a few different psychiatrists. He thought they were responsible for her condition. He never figured out that Vanessa had a lot to do with her own condition. If she didn't want to quit, no one could help her.

Her mother was smarter, though, when she put Vanessa in the last rehab. Before she entered Newtown, her mother told her, "Unless you quit, you're not coming home. If you can't quit, I don't want you in this house."

Her mother could afford to do anything for her now.

Usually when I got out of rehab or out of jail, I wouldn't have any money in my pocket. I'd go back to hanging around the street, prostituting myself and selling drugs. This time I didn't have to do that.

One night Vanessa and I had had gone outside and were sitting by the pool in her yard watching the sunset. She talked to me more that night than she ever had before.

"I used to sit around this pool with my friend," she said. "We used to sleep over at each other's houses. She didn't even drink. Her mother worried about her, though, and put her away in private school. I didn't want her to start doing that either. When I took drugs, I'd only do it with my boyfriend, Paul. His parents are very rich. After I started to drink and take drugs, my mom would try to isolate me from him, but she was drinking a lot then too. My father had a girlfriend and he and my mom were always having arguments. They finally got divorced and my mom fell apart then. I'd stay with my grandmother in her big home in Greenwich."

Vanessa told me she had to get sober so she could show her mom she wouldn't do drugs and alcohol anymore. She knew she could no longer live like that. She realized that she'd been wrong, she said, and that when she drank and did drugs, she didn't know who she was.

I knew what she meant.

Vanessa told me she thought her mom really loved her and had just wanted her to quit drugs and alcohol.

"I know those things were not doing me any favors," she said, "and what I did to my mom all these years, I did because of the money we had. Everything was so convenient. Every time I asked for money, she or my dad would give it to me. They never asked what I did with it. Paul and I would go to New York. We could drink there, and then we'd come back to Connecticut drunk. My dad caught me once and that's how I first got sent for help.

I hurt my parents terribly. I know that. I've realized they love me. I understand now."

Vanessa was so much different than I. She had money. She could do whatever she wanted to do. Me, I had no money. I couldn't do what she could do.

I looked at her and I felt hurt because her mother and father would do anything for her to get better. I wished I had that support.

I didn't have the money she had. I didn't have the love she had.

I just had excuses.

I was different.

I felt that I had been taking drugs and doing alcohol so much longer than she, and that I was beyond help. If I had had someone to help me stop and to give me emotional support, like she had, I think I could have gotten off drugs and alcohol too. But I didn't have any support. I knew that.

"Listen," Vanessa told me one day, "You're a beautiful woman. You have a good heart. You're good enough for any man, and one day you will find a man who really loves you. Don't turn him down. As long as you love each other, that's what counts. You can't worry about anything else. Now that you've gotten sober and gotten to be yourself again, you don't want to go back to where you were before. We've both been in rehab for a long time. I know you and I have done some bad things, but please don't go back to where you were before. You take care of yourself. You know, you're still young. There's still a lot of things you can do out there."

"You know, Vanessa, that's what my grandma always says too."

"There's nothing wrong with you. Look what you've done with me. You came to me and wanted to help me even though I didn't want to talk to anyone. You did talk to me and I started expressing myself finally."

I gave her a hug.

We had been talking together in her bedroom for most of the night and by now it was late.

"Good night, Vanessa," I said.

"Good night, Gina. I love you," she said to me.

After she left my room, I started crying uncontrollably. I realized I could have married Christopher and that he had loved me. He did so much for me, but I just couldn't do it, not just because of sex, but because I worried about hurting him too.

If I had married him, I would have a nice home, maybe not like this one, but a nice one. Christopher worked hard and made good money.

But I could never have children for him because I had done such heavy drugs and alcohol for such a long time.

When I got up the next morning, I looked in the mirror and my eyes were all puffy from crying so hard the night before. They looked like I had been drinking. I went to the refrigerator and got some ice to put on them.

Vanessa came into the kitchen and asked if I was all right. "Your eyes are all swollen," she said.

"Yeah, "I said. "I've got a little allergy to dogs." She had two dogs in the house.

"Oh," she said.

"My eyes are like this most of the time if I'm around animals," I said to her.

"You never told me that," she said.

"It's okay. They don't hurt. They're just swollen. It'll go away soon."

She told me her friends were going to take her out to lunch that day and she wanted me to go with them. I said maybe she should go and I'd just hang around there and sit by the pool and relax.

"No. You're coming with me," she said.

Later we rented a movie and went back home and watched it. I shouldn't have. It was a love story and it brought all my thoughts about Christopher.

I felt sorry for myself.

After the movie I went up to my bedroom, but Vanessa asked if she could come in and talk to me.

She asked me what was going on.

I told her that I had gotten pregnant by Christopher when we had first been in the tub together, but I never told him. I flew down to Florida and got an abortion. My cousin had loaned me the money and taken me to the doctor.

I had wanted so badly to keep the baby, but the doctor had told me I had done so many drugs and drunk so much alcohol that if I had had kids, they might not be right.

My mother had warned me too. She said that she had drunk a lot when she was younger, while she was pregnant, and none of her three kids had turned out right. She told me she never, ever wanted to see another human being like me or like my brother again.

I told Vanessa that after I had left Christopher in the middle of that night, I had started taking drugs and drinking again.

I had just wanted to be normal, like everybody else, but I knew I was going to suffer the rest of my life instead. I knew, though, that I'd brought it all on myself.

She hugged me and told me she was sorry. She could imagine how I felt. We both cried and hugged each other.

I told her that I had one friend who would always talk to me, always help me, no matter what I had done. I said I was going to go see him after I got home. He was my guardian angel.

She told me I was a beautiful girl and she knew I could turn my life around.

After she left my room, I closed my eyes and realized I felt relaxed. I felt no tension around Vanessa.

I went to sleep quickly.

The next morning Vanessa invited me out for breakfast and to go shopping.

After breakfast we went to a little boutique where she bought some things for herself and then asked me if I liked a certain coat.

"Try it in on. I think it will look good on you," she said.

"I can't do that. I don't have any money. I don't even have a credit card."

"Please go try it," she repeated. "I just want to see it on you."

She came into the dressing room and watched me put it on. She said I should get it and she went and picked up a couple blouses for me and bought them and the coat as well. I told her not to do that.

"I have clothes at home," I said.

"But not these clothes!" she said, holding them up.

I said she shouldn't do that, but she insisted.

Inside I was happy. I needed a coat.

She had a big heart. I thanked her and we went home.

I knew I couldn't stay there any longer, so I told Vanessa the next day that I was leaving. She told me to come back any time.

Their cook was going to prepare a special dinner for me and she called him on the way home to let him know what I wanted. We stopped at a pastry store too and bought two different boxes of sweets.

"When you quit drinking, you crave sweets. I know," she said.

That night her mother asked me if I had been having a good time. I told her I had and she kissed me on the forehead.

"Why don't you stay a little longer?" she asked.

"No. I told my grandmother I would be home tomorrow. I really appreciate your inviting me here. I did enjoy myself."

Her mother told me how much she would miss me.

We went into the dining room and sat down to eat. It was steak and lobster, just for me. Her mother looked across the table at the two of us and said, "You two look so much alike you could be sisters."

We all laughed, and Vanessa's mother asked me again if I couldn't stay for a few more days.

I said no.

When I left the next day, I told Vanessa I was sure she was going to be all right.

I wasn't so sure about me.

I had seen what strong will power Vanessa had and I wondered if I had it too. Deep down I was afraid that all the problems in my life would soon come to the surface again.

"Don't forget to write," Vanessa said. "My mom and I are going to Europe for a bit, but when I get to London, I'll write you. But I'll call before I go."

We hugged each other and said how much we'd miss each other.

After I got on the train, I thought I'd take a nap. I closed my eyes and started thinking of my guardian angel. I missed him. He was so nice to me.

Whenever I had left him, I wasn't thinking of myself. I was thinking of him.

I didn't want to hurt him.

Chapter Fifteen

When I got home, my grandma asked me where I'd been.

I hadn't written. I hadn't called. She didn't know where I was. I gave her a big hug and told her I had gone to spend some time with a friend.

"You look good," she told me. "You've never looked so good."

My grandma told me she needed a lot of things for the house, but she didn't have any money. She couldn't cash the check she had because she couldn't drive any longer and my mom hadn't been by for weeks. My grandma didn't know if she'd gone on vacation or what.

I didn't have any money in my pockets either.

I told my grandma I would call a taxi and we could go to a bank so she could cash her check and then we'd go to a grocery store. We could pay the cab after we were done.

While we waited for the cab, I unpacked my bag so I could put my jeans on. I still had on shorts and wanted to change before we went out.

I noticed an envelope buried within all the clothes in my bag.

It was full of money.

"Maybe my girlfriend put it in my bag for me," I told my grandma.

"Maybe it fell from heaven," my grandma said.

I called Vanessa and asked her if she had put it in my bag.

"Yes, my ma had given me some money for you and I stuffed it in your things. I wanted it to be a surprise and I didn't think you'd take it if I just handed it to you. I figured you could use it until you found some work for yourself."

"How am I going to repay you?" I asked her.

"You're not. That's yours."

"I don't know what to say. Thank you."

I got a job as a waitress at a local restaurant. No drugs. No alcohol. Just dishes. I felt good working.

One night a man came into the restaurant and he looked just like my brother. His haircut, his eyes, even his eyebrows.

He must have thought that I liked him because I was staring at him so.

But he looked exactly like my brother.

He sat down at one of the tables and after he had finished his dinner, he went and sat in the bar. He kept watching me.

I found out later his name was Renaldo. I think he was half Cuban. He had light skin and dark hair and he was very handsome.

We didn't talk that night. We just looked at each other.

He must have come from a good family. His nails were well manicured. His hair was short. He dressed nicely. He had style and I had never stared at anybody like that before. He looked perfect.

I wanted to know what he did.

Even though I had been clean for a while then, every time a guy had seen me, he wanted to get to know me, but when he found out who I was, he just wanted to get away.

I'm not sure how many times Renaldo had come to the restaurant when I wasn't there, but he came in more and more often. Sometimes he'd talk, sometimes not. Often he'd just sit and watch me. He always came in alone.

I said to the other waitress one night, "You see that man over there? He comes here a lot?"

"Yeah, used to be once in a while, but recently he's come in all the time."

I was lying in bed one night and I was thinking about him, but I felt he was not a guy for me because he was too good, too good looking.

What would he do with me, I thought. I didn't dress nicely. I didn't go to beauty salons. I didn't do much of anything for myself. I told myself I shouldn't be staring at him like I had been.

When he came in the next time, I just looked away.

I wasn't like most girls. I was lost in a lot of ways. I liked the job that I had and I liked working. People were nice to me, but I was mixed up about a lot of things in my life still.

I started to work longer and longer hours and I was getting too little sleep. I was beginning to wear myself out. I was starting to get sick.

I wanted to stay away from Renaldo.

One night he asked me if I needed a ride home.

I got chills.

"No, thank you," I said. "There's a girl who works here. Gigi. She drives me home. We live together."

"Okay," he said. "Maybe I'll see you tomorrow."

I didn't want to get in a stranger's car. I didn't want to go near somebody I didn't know. I was scared. I always looked behind my back and to my left and right.

I was probably paranoid from withdrawal. I hadn't had any drugs for three months.

One day Renaldo came in and just stood at the door to the restaurant for a long time. I tried not to stare at him and I busied myself with what I was supposed to be doing.

He came up to me and asked me again to go out.

I told him I couldn't go out with him because he was a client of the restaurant. My boss had warned me about that and I didn't want anything to happen to my job. I had to work to support myself, I told him.

He didn't say anything.

A few weeks later he sent me roses with a note inside saying he would really like to get together.

"I would like to take you dinner," he wrote. He had signed his name on the card.

It was sweet.

I told my girlfriend Gigi that the flowers were from the guy who came here so often. She said he was always looking at me and that she thought he liked me.

One night he came into the restaurant very late. He asked me if he could sit at my table and I told him that if he wanted to have dinner, I'd take his order right then because we were going to close in a minute.

He ordered an appetizer and his meal and his desert all at once and said he'd have tea to drink. Then he asked me if I had received his flowers.

I said I had, but told him he shouldn't do that. I told him I really didn't want to have a relationship with a client of the restaurant.

He said he didn't think it had anything to do with that.

I told him I really didn't have any time. I couldn't date. I was too busy. I was tired when I went home and I worked in the day sometimes and on weekends too.

I told him that as nice a looking man as he was, he must have a lot of other girlfriends.

He told me he didn't.

Finally I just told him that he wouldn't want me. He didn't know me or my background. I didn't know him either, I said.

He told me I wasn't giving him a chance to know me, and he asked me again if he could give me a ride home.

I told him I didn't want to get in his car because I didn't know him and he didn't know me.

"But how am I going to get to know you and how are you going to get to know me?" he asked. "You're still not giving me a chance."

"That's true," I said. "But I can't get in your car."

"What's the matter?" he asked. "Is there something wrong with me?"

"No. There's nothing wrong with you. I just don't know you. Today you hear so many stories about what happens out there. You understand, don't you?"

None of this should have been happening with a guy in the restaurant. My boss would fire me if he found out.

I wished I'd met him somewhere else and not there, but I knew he wasn't going to give up, no matter what I said.

I repeated that I couldn't date him. I had no time.

"Well, how about just dinner some night?" he asked.

"I don't have any days off," I lied to him. "I just started this job and I don't have any days off."

"I could just take you to breakfast to get to know you—and you me—a little better."

"I keep telling you, I can't," I said. "Maybe one day, but I don't know when."

I let him eat his meal at the table by himself.

"I think you're afraid," he finally said to me, "but I don't know what you're afraid of. Here's my card. If you can, give me a ring."

I looked back over at his table later and he was gone.

I didn't see him for several weeks and I thought he was never going to come back. I still had his card, but I wouldn't call him.

He worked for the government, but I wasn't sure what he did. His card just gave his phone number, his name and the address of his office. I thought maybe he was a spy.

Finally he came back into the restaurant one day.

"How are you doing?" I asked him. "I haven't seen you for awhile."

"I had gone to see my parents. They live in Miami," he said. "I still would really like to get to know you. We should get together for dinner, okay?"

I kept telling him I couldn't go to dinner with him and I couldn't go out with him.

Then, one night, just to get him off my back, I told him that maybe sometime when I wasn't busy, I would let him know ahead of time and we could go out to dinner.

I didn't feel I would be very good company for him and I didn't want someone trying to figure out why I was the way I was. Those days I could hardly concentrate on any one thing. I couldn't think clearly. Sometimes I was happy, sometimes I wasn't, and sometimes I couldn't even pay attention to another person when they were sitting right across from me.

How could I go out to dinner with him?

I just wanted to be by myself for a while still.

I didn't want to hurt his feelings, but I couldn't really spend time with him or anyone else at that time.

One night at the restaurant Renaldo begged Gigi to give him our phone number and on my next day off, he called me.

"This is Renaldo," he said.

"I didn't give you my phone number," he said. "Where'd you get it?"

"From the girl who works with you," he said.

"Oh. How are you doing?"

"Fine. How are you doing?"

"Fine," I said. "Today's a day off, but I've got to run errands."

"Could we go to dinner?" he asked.

"No."

"Okay. Some other time then."

"Sure. I'll let you know."

"Okay. Maybe I'll see you tomorrow at the restaurant.

The next night he said to me, "I've just figured out why you don't want to date me. It's because I'm Cuban. You're prejudiced."

I felt terrible.

"No, no. It's not that," I said. "I used to have a lot of friends from Cuba. They're nice people. Don't say I'm prejudiced. I like everybody, all kinds, anybody."

I was still feeling bad after a few days and so I called him at his office.

"I would like to talk to you" I said. "We can go to a coffee shop this evening. I'm not prejudiced."

"You're not, huh?" he said. I thought for a moment I heard him laugh. "I want to take you to a restaurant, not a coffee shop. I know a place you'll love. What time do you want me to pick you up?"

"You don't have to pick me up," I said. "I can meet you there."

"No. I'll pick you up. Gigi told me where you live."

I told him okay.

He picked me up that night in his Corvette and took me to the restaurant.

His car was good looking, but it made a lot of noise and he drove fast. I asked him to slow down. I told him I never had been in a sports car in my whole life and I supposed if you had one, you had to drive it fast.

"Not really," he said and slowed down. "Maybe that's why you don't want to go in anybody's car. You're probably just nervous."

He was smiling.

We got to the restaurant and I was hungry because I hadn't eaten all day. He ordered wine for himself and asked if I wanted any.

"No, I don't drink wine," I told him. "Just soft drinks."

"You don't have to drink the whole bottle," he said. "Don't worry. Just have a glass."

I said no.

"You can have it," he insisted. "I'll order glasses for both of us. What would you like to eat?"

"You come here a lot," I said. "Why don't you order for us?"

He asked me if I wanted an appetizer and when I said yes, he asked me if I liked clams or shrimp. I told him I liked shrimp cocktails and he ordered one for me and mussels and clams for himself.

"You look worried," he said to me.

"I haven't been out on a date for a long time," I said. "Bear with me."

I kept wondering what to say to him. I couldn't tell this man my background. He wouldn't want to hear that.

So I didn't say anything. I just sat there trying to enjoy myself.

"You know, you're the only girl who's ever said 'no' to me? Why is that? Every time I asked a girl to date, I had a date with them in a day or two. But not you. Months and months have gone by. You've always said no. Can you tell me why?"

"Sure. Because I'm tired after work. Before I moved here and started working, I had been kind of sick."

"How long have you lived here?"

"Not long," I said.

"Where were you before?"

"I lived in Derby. Sometimes I'd go to Florida and visit my friends. I'd stay there for a few days and then travel a little bit, but not any more. I haven't actually gone there for a long time."

"Well, it's probably time for you to go back," he said. "With me."

Over the next few weeks I started going out with Renaldo more and working at the restaurant less.

One night, when I walked in to work, my boss called me into his office and told me he was letting me go.

"The customers love you, Gina, but you can't put in the time we need. I'm sorry."

I told Renaldo and he said, "Great! Now we can go to Florida."

The next day he called me and said he was on vacation and he was coming over.

He arrived at my apartment a few minutes later and pulled two airline tickets to Miami out if his blazer pocket.

"We leave in the morning," he said.

"Oh, my God, Renaldo!" was all I could say.

Chapter Sixteen

The next night we were walking on the beach near his parents' home in Miami and he was holding my hand.

"I feel so good with you," he said, "no matter what we're doing. Look at me, Gina."

We stopped walking and I looked right into his eyes.

"I want to tell you something," he said. "Sometimes parents are never happy with their son's or daughter's friends or their fiancées. They think they're not good enough for them. My mom acts that way. I know that she's my mother and I can't change her, but she can't change me either. Don't worry about her."

He hugged me tightly. He touched my hair and took my face and held it to his and kissed me. I kissed him back.

He knew how to kiss.

I put my head on his chest. He felt warm against my cheek.

"You must understand," I said to him. "I don't like it when someone is unhappy about me. I've made people unhappy my whole life. I don't want to do that anymore."

I knew his mother hadn't liked me when she met me that afternoon. She'd been sitting with a crowd of people in her living room and she barely said hello to me. I remembered being called a tramp and a whore by Jamie's mom. I felt bad.

"You sound like you've had a tough life," Renaldo said.

"Yes."

"Tell me," he said gently.

"No. Maybe another time."

We walked back along the beach.

"I don't care if your mom doesn't like me," I told him. "Let's just say good night to her, okay."

We went back to his house and into their kitchen. His parents will still up, but their company had all gone to bed.

His mother asked me, "Do you want a cup of coffee, sweetheart? Would you like some cake? I have some delicious cake. It's homemade. Please sit down."

I sat down with Renaldo, his mother and his father at the table.

His mother told me that she was sorry about how she'd acted earlier.

She had been so busy entertaining her friends—she hadn't seen them for years and they had come all the way from Cuba—and she hadn't sat down with me and talked with me the first thing when I had come in earlier. She apologized again and just said that she had had a tough day that day because she had been so busy preparing for these people to come.

"I understand," I told her.

"Gina, right? Gina, did you and Renaldo have a nice walk?"

I told her I felt like I'd been in heaven walking on the warm beach at night, the ocean splashing against our toes.

She looked at me strangely for a second. Then she looked at Renaldo. She knew Renaldo liked me. Maybe she was jealous. I couldn't tell.

I did know that Renaldo was her only son, and I didn't think she wanted me to take her only son away from her.

Then I noticed she had changed her mind again in an instant. She was smiling at me.

"Are you enjoying yourself here?" she asked me.

"Very much so," I said. "And you have a very beautiful place here. I've never been to a house like this before in my life. It's like you'd see in the movies. It's like a castle."

She was laughing.

"Tomorrow I can spend a little time with you," she said. "Do you get up early in the morning?"

"Yes," I said.

"Why don't you get up early and I'll meet you in the kitchen. Renaldo will show you where the kitchen is before you go to sleep. In fact, he can show you all around."

I finished my cake and Renaldo took me to the main house. She had beautiful furniture and beautiful rugs, all so colorful. I had never seen anything like it. What looked like very expensive oil paintings were hung across the walls.

"This isn't just like a castle," I told Renaldo. "It is a castle. These paintings are beautiful."

We went upstairs. I asked to use the bathroom, and I went to wash my hands in the sink. It looked like it was made of gold. I didn't dare ask Renaldo if it was.

We went out onto the second floor deck to look at the ocean. The water and the sky were beautiful, both so clear, so warm.

Renaldo told me he would like to have a house like this someday when he settled down. He squeezed my hand.

"I've seen a lot of big houses, houses like castles," I said to Renaldo, "but never a house like this. Your mom knows how to decorate. It's beautiful. Can we sit here a little bit."

We sat down on two chaise lounges on the deck and stared out at the ocean.

"You know," Renaldo said, "I think you're tired. You've had a hard day today."

He got up and put his hand out and helped me up out of the chair and we walked downstairs. There were so many rooms in the house, I lost count of them. Each was decorated beautifully and each had paintings on its walls. The lamps all looked like they were antiques. There were ornate porcelain vases throughout the rooms and he said his mother had collected them all. Everything looked expensive.

I went and said good night to his mother and then Renaldo walked me to the guest house. He asked me if I needed anything, but said the guest house had everything: a kitchen, a bathroom, a bedroom.

"I'm fine," I said. "When you leave, I'm going to soak myself in the tub."

"That's a good idea!" he said.

The bathroom in the guest house was so big it had a double bath in it. There was a Jacuzzi too. Renaldo turned the TV on for me in the living room. It was a huge, big screen TV. I felt like I was in a movie theatre.

"I've never seen anything like this," I said to Renaldo.

Renaldo sat down and was watching the news. I thought he should leave, but I didn't say that. I just let him sit there.

"Maybe I shouldn't take my bath while you're still here," I said to him.

"Why? Just go check and see if you need anything in the bathroom. I know where everything is."

I went and started my bath. I didn't want to take a shower. I wanted to soak myself. My back was bothering me because I had been sitting in the plane for so long. I had been nervous flying, too, and had been holding my body tense. I ran the water and got the temperature the way I wanted it.

When the water was ready, I slid my body down into the bathtub and thought again that I'd gone to heaven. The water was so warm.

Renaldo called into me and asked if I was all right. I must have moaned, it felt so good. I told him I was just fine.

I was tired, and I closed my eyes and just lay in the tub for a while. I must have fallen asleep. I woke up to Renaldo calling out again and asking if I was all right. I yelled back that I had dozed off in the tub.

"My God!" he said. "You don't want to drown yourself in there, do you?"

"Drown myself in the bathtub?!" I asked and laughed.

"Well, you never know. Say, do you want me to come in and wash your back? There's some bubble bath there I can pour in for you."

"No, no. I'm fine," I said. I didn't want him to come near me.

I continued to soak myself and when I got out, I looked down at my legs. They must have gotten too hot in the water because they were all red, like two lobster claws. It hadn't felt that hot.

Renaldo came in and took a towel and started to dry my hair. "Do you want me to blow dry it?" he asked.

I told him I hadn't washed it because it took such a long time to dry. "I have such thick hair," I said. "I'm too tired to do that tonight. Tomorrow morning I will."

"I could help you," he said.

My God, I said to myself.

"I'm fine," I said to him.

I went out in the living room and sat on the couch. He was looking at my legs.

"How come your feet are so red?" he asked.

"I think I turned the water on too hot," I said.

"Are you sure you're okay?" he asked. "You've cooked yourself."

"Like a lobster," I said.

We were both laughing.

"You shouldn't make the water that hot. You'll get dizzy," he said.

"Well, you know I did just close my eyes and fall asleep. It felt so good."

I went and looked in my suitcase. I didn't have a nightgown. All I had were tee shirts. I didn't want to put one on while he was still there. They were old and worn, but it was all I could find at home when I packed.

I sat on the couch with just a bathrobe on. He asked me if I was comfortable and I told him I was fine.

"Didn't you bring any nightgowns?" he asked.

"I forgot," I said.

"What are you going to wear, then?" he asked.

"If I just have a tee shirt to sleep in, I'm fine," I told him. I figured he'd never heard something like that, to wear a tee shirt instead of a nightgown. I was embarrassed and I laughed a little.

"Do you want a tee shirt? I'll go get you a tee shirt," he said.

"Okay," I said. The guest house had air conditioning and I was beginning to get cold.

"What else do you need? Do you want some of my underwear too?"

"No, no. Just bring me a tee shirt and I'll be fine." I figured if it were his, even if it had holes, he wouldn't make fun of it.

But I didn't think his tee shirts had holes in them.

I was sitting on the couch and watching TV. The sofa felt so soft I just lay down and closed my eyes. I was still tired and I was relaxed after my bath. I felt like I had taken a tranquilizer.

Renaldo came back in and handed me what looked like a brand new white tee shirt.

"Go get comfortable," he said.

"I'm fine," I said. "I'll keep this robe on until I go to bed because it's cold in here."

"Why didn't you just ask me to turn the air conditioning down? I can do that, you know."

"Renaldo, do you know what I'm trying to say? I'm ready for bed. I mean, for sleep. Do you know what I mean?"

"I could see that that's what you were trying to say. Every time you say something, you say to me, 'You know what I mean?' What does that mean?!"

We laughed.

"I think I should go," Renaldo said.

He kept sitting there, though, watching his show, Sixty Minutes. He liked to watch it, I could tell, so I just let him be. I was really cold, even though he'd turned the air conditioner lower and even though I still had the robe on.

I got up and walked over in front of him. He was sitting in one of the chairs.

"You know, I'm enjoying myself here," I said to him. "Thank you for bringing me here."

He stood and grabbed the robe I had on and he covered my neck up tightly with it. He looked down at me and I stood up on my tiptoes and kissed him on his cheek.

He picked me up and carried me over to the sofa to sit on his lap.

"I thought you were thin when I held you, but you're heavy," he said.

"What do you mean?" I asked. "That means I'm fat?"

"No. I just didn't think you were so heavy. How much do you weigh?"

"I weigh a hundred and twenty-five pounds," I told him. "I'm just short. That's why I look chubby."

"You're just my size," he said, "and you are not chubby."

After I had been sitting in his lap for a while, he picked me up and carried me into my bed. His arms were solid and strong. I thought he must exercise a lot because he was so firm.

He laid me down onto the bed and told me to take my robe off.

"I'll tuck you in," he said.

Oh, my God, I said to myself.

I slid under the covers and handed him out my robe.

He said he was going to let me go to sleep.

"I'd better leave here before anything happens," he said.

"What's going to happen?" I asked.

"Nothing," he said.

He gave me a kiss, said he'd see me in the morning and left.

At the door he asked me what time I wanted him to come back and wake me.

"Not too early," I said.

"Sure," he said. "Have sweet dreams."

"You have strong arms," I told him. "You could hurt me with those arms just holding me."

"Don't get smart," he said. "Good night."

"Good night."

I fell asleep within minutes.

I hadn't felt that tired in a long, long time and I slept right through to the morning.

Chapter Seventeen

In the morning, when I opened my eyes, I thought I was still dreaming.

Everything was so beautiful. Everything was brand new, the curtains, the rugs. The bed, I realized, was huge. I hadn't really noticed the night before.

I got out of bed and opened the window and went out onto the deck. I smelled the salt air. I could see the ocean. I felt good, but it didn't seem it could be true.

I'd only seen that kind of place in the movies when I was little. I'd never thought I'd be in a place like that. Now, standing there, I wondered if my dreams were coming true.

I went over and sat down on one of the chairs and let the sunshine come down on my face for a while. It felt good and I went back inside to get my dark glasses so I could stay out there for a while.

I didn't know anyone could live like this. It was too rich and my background was too poor. For so long I had only lived day by day with my bottle and my syringe. I kept telling myself this wasn't real life. Or maybe it was.

I sat in that chair and thought about what I had been doing with my life and I started to feel bad. If I only knew how to forget my past, maybe I wouldn't feel this bad any more. But my past was in my head and I couldn't get away from it.

I felt like I wanted a drink.

Everywhere I went there was liquor. Last night there was a lot of liquor on their dinner table. They drank champagne and wine at dinner. When I looked at it, my body started to sweat. I had to close my eyes and pretend I hadn't seen it, but I couldn't help it. If I had started to drink, I wouldn't stop. I'd be drinking it through the night and day.

I heard the phone ringing inside. It was about ten o'clock. It must be Renaldo.

"Good morning," he said when I answered. "Are you hungry?"

"Yes, I am," I said.

"I'm going to come over now," he said.

I went and unlocked the door. I was still in my robe when he came in. He was wearing shorts and I whistled when he walked in.

"What legs!" I said.

"What's with your legs?" he asked.

"I'm not talking about my legs. I'm talking about yours," I said.

"You're funny," he said. "Why don't you get ready now? We'll have some breakfast. What do you want to do today?"

"I want to stay in bed all day."

"I don't think so. What a waste! I'd like to go someplace. I'll take you round and show you some things you've never seen before."

I was worried about what I was going to wear. I only had a few jeans and a couple blouses with me. Renaldo said he'd never seen anybody travel so light. I had a tiny suitcase. I just didn't have many clothes.

"Let's go over to Palm Beach," Renaldo said. "You'll like it. It's very busy and there's lots of people, if you like that."

"Sure," I said. "I would love to walk around there."

"Let's leave now and then we can stop somewhere and get breakfast on the way," he said. "My mom's not up yet. She goes to bed very late, especially last night after all that company."

I still had my robe on and I walked up very close to him and gave him a hug.

"What's that about? Are you okay?" he asked me.

"I'm fine." I hugged him again. He put his arm around me and stroked my hair with his hand. He started running his fingers through my hair.

"God, you sure do have a lot of hair," he said.

He kept his hands on the back of my head and put his cheek next to mine.

"You're so warm," I said. It felt so good when I stood next to him. I felt like I really wanted to have him and then just lie in bed with him. That was all that was on my mind.

"Well, let's go," he said. "If you want, we can come home early and you can take a nap."

He just wanted to go, go, go. He didn't want to stay in one place for too long.

"Okay, let's go," I said. "I don't have any dresses with me, though."

"What do you want a dress for? Everybody wears jeans. Do you have shorts?"

"No, just regular jeans." I had a nice figure, my mom always told me, and whatever I threw on, I looked good in.

We walked outside and over toward the main house.

"The car's out in back," Renaldo said.

Suddenly I saw their pool and I just wanted to jump in. I didn't have a swimming suit with me. I had thought of that last night, but didn't know what to do about it. I thought maybe I could find something when we walked around Palm Beach. I put my fingers down into the pool water. It was warm, perfect.

There were a lot of little kids in the pool and I told Renaldo that when we got home, I might jump in the pool. He said he'd already been swimming before I got up.

"What time did you get up?" I asked him.

"Seven o'clock. I've trained myself," he said.

We walked around to the garage and I saw his family had three Mercedes Benz. We got into the black convertible and Renaldo put the top down.

"Oh, God," I said. The interior was all soft red leather.

We drove out and over to the thruway. His neighborhood was full of beautiful houses and I felt like I was in a different world. I didn't know if it was real life, but it wasn't real life for me.

While we were driving, Renaldo looked over at me and told me again that I looked worried.

"No, I'm not," I said. "I'm enjoying myself."

"I hope so," he said.

It was a little windy and my hair was flying all over the place.

"You know, when I look at you and your hair is off your face, you look differ-ent," he said. "You're very pretty. You have a very pretty face."

He always was complimenting me and he knew what to say to me to make me feel good.

He spotted a restaurant and asked me if I liked pancakes. I said sure and we decided to stop and go in. It was The Pancake Club and it was crowded.

While we were eating our breakfast, he asked me if I wanted to walk around or ride around when we got to Palm Beach. I told him I'd rather walk around, but that I needed to get a swimsuit while we were there.

"When's the last time you came down to Florida?" he asked me.

"When I was little," I lied. "My grandma's friend lived around here. I was probably about seven years old. I still remember where we went and what we did. We didn't travel a lot, though, because both my parents worked. When I was growing up I lived mostly with my aunt or my grandma because my mother worked in the evenings. I had two brothers. They always were fighting, maybe just because they were young and didn't know what they were doing. My mom didn't want me to stay home with them. I wasn't interested in staying home any-way. I liked to go out with the other kids my age. My grandma took care of me because she was home all day. When I was growing up, I was practically always on my own, always going places. I had a lot of friends then."

I decided I'd better just stop talking right there.

We ate the rest of our breakfast quickly and silently and left.

When we stood up and went to pay, everybody in the restaurant seemed to stare at us. I didn't know why, maybe because my hair was so bushy. I didn't have a lot of makeup on. Just lipstick.

Outside Renaldo opened my car door for me.

"You attract quite a bit of attention," he said. He had a smile on his face.

I hadn't meant to have people look at me.

We got in the Mercedes and he asked me if I didn't want him to put the top up.

"No. I like it," I said. "I like it when the wind is blowing against my face."

It was a nice drive to Palm Beach.

Renaldo said he had friends up in Palm Beach, but he didn't think I was interested in just sitting around and talking with people. He wasn't, I knew.

"We'll walk around," he said.

There were a lot of jewelry stores on Worth Avenue and we looked in the windows. In one there was a beautiful diamond, a huge rock, and I just passed by. I didn't even want to go in. With what little money I had, they wouldn't have let me in the door, I thought.

I finally went in one boutique. I told Renaldo it looked like my price range and I thought they might have an inexpensive swimsuit.

Renaldo kept picking up things from around the shop and telling me to try them on. He picked up a blouse, some shorts, a skirt. I went to try them on and came back out to show him.

"Wow. I like that," he said.

I put them aside.

"Do you want to try this?" he said, holding up another pair of shorts and a blouse.

I really didn't want him spending any money because if anything happened to us, I would feel guilty.

I went back and tried on a nice dress. It was pretty short.

"Wow!" he said when I came out. "That looks great on you. You really know how to pick a color that matches your skin and hair."

He then gave me quite a few other dresses to try on. I put one on to show him, a light one made out of silk. He told me it was very pretty.

"I want you to get two dresses you can wear," he said. "I think tomorrow night my mom is having some kind of party, her mother's birthday or some university thing. I forget. I'd better call her. Maybe I'll get something for her too."

I picked out a couple pair of shorts, a blouse and two dresses.

He said, "That's all?"

"You don't want to buy the store, do you?"

He was laughing, but said, "You should pick up a few more things."

"No, that's great. That's all I need." I really didn't want him to spend a lot of money. I knew these clothes were expensive because I'd looked at the tags. Most of the dresses were around two hundred dollars, some as much as five hundred.

I couldn't wait to leave because I was afraid he'd pick up something else and make me try it on. He would insist I get it if I put it on. I could tell.

"Let's go," I said. "All I need now is to get a swimming suit."

"That's fine with me," he said. "Tonight I want to take you to a disco. I love to go there. Do you like to dance?"

"Yes, I do," I said.

"Can I pick out just one dress for you then for the disco? I know what you'll look good in."

He went and looked around the boutique and I just stood there waiting for him to find something. He came back with a dress over his arm.

"I want you to try this on first to make sure you're comfortable in it and you like it."

I put it on and ran my hands over it. It was so smooth. The skirt came up over my knees, not too short, not too long. I loved it. It was the perfect length. I came out from the dressing room and all the girls in the shop went "Wow!"

"You have the figure," one said. "You have the legs. You'd look good in anything, but especially in this dress. It's beautiful on you."

Renaldo said, "You can wear it tonight. You can wear it anywhere! It looks stunning on you. Do you like it?"

"I love it," I said.

Renaldo went and paid for it.

I was so happy. I'd never had a dress like that in my life. My family would never have bought me a dress like this, not even my grandma."

Next we went into another shop to get a swimsuit. I asked him to pick one out. He was a good shopper and he knew exactly what color would match my skin.

He went around the shop and picked out four or five different suits.

"Listen," I said. "I don't need five different suits. I'll pick up two so I can have one extra to change into. These dry quickly because the material is so thin. I don't know about this bikini, though, Renaldo. It's not going to cover much of me. I don't think your mom would approve."

He picked up another suit that wasn't a bikini, but it was low in back and even lower in front. It was sexy and I liked it.

"Maybe I'll get one of those," I said, "and maybe one bikini."

He told me to get more than that, but I said no so he went to the cashier and paid for the two I had. We left the store.

"Maybe we should go back home and go swimming," I said. "We can stay outside by the pool and hang around in the sun. Your pool's so beautiful."

"Sure," Renaldo said. "Good idea."

We drove home and he and I went to the guesthouse. I unpacked my things and went into the bathroom to try on one of the dresses.

"You know, I'm not sure of this one dress," I called out to him.

"Okay," he said. "Make sure. If you don't like it, we can go back there tomorrow and exchange it."

"I'll try it on and show you."

I took off my jeans and blouse and put the dress on and went out into the living room.

"It looks beautiful to me," Renaldo said.

I'd never worn a dress like that before and I began to feel a little sad that I hadn't. The dress was so pretty. It had cost over five hundred dollars.

"Renaldo, I want to tell you the truth. I think this dress is too expensive."

"No. It was one of the cheapest dresses of that kind that they had there. That's Palm Beach for you. Why don't you keep it? You can wear it tonight if my mom has a lot of people over. You could wear it to the disco. There's a nice club we'll go to not far from here. You'll like it."

I went over and kissed him.

"It looks very pretty on you, you know that, right?" he said.

"Yes. Too beautiful for me. I've never had a dress like this in my whole life."

"Enjoy it," he said.

I gave him a hug and another kiss. We kissed each other and he started rubbing my back.

The sleeves on the dress were satiny thin and they hung down smoothly and nicely, but I hadn't fastened the back of the dress when I was in the bathroom. I reached down for his hand and the dress fell off. All I had on was a thong. I don't like bras.

He couldn't control himself.

Neither could I.

I wanted to be close with him, but I was sad because we weren't really thinking about what we were doing. Everything was automatic.

We didn't even speak a word.

Chapter Eighteen

I lay my head on his chest. I kissed him and told him he was so warm.

"I'll keep you warm, too," he said.

It was midnight and we were still in bed. We'd been there all night and I told him I was getting a little hungry.

"Me, too," he said. "Put your clothes on and we'll go to the main house."

I was getting a plate of food for us from the refrigerator in the kitchen of the main house when I noticed the wine and beer on the bottom shelf. I stared and stared at it. I thought maybe I'd have just a little beer or maybe just a glass of wine. It was the perfect time for a drink.

Finally I said to myself, "No, you don't" and I took a Coke instead.

We sat in the kitchen eating and listening to a Spanish station on the radio.

After we finished, I got up from the able and turned the music up. I pulled him up and started dancing with him. It was a slow song and I put my head on his chest.

"I can hear your heart beating," I told him. "You've got a strong heart."

"I am strong," he said, "when I'm close to you."

It felt so good to be next to him.

We went out and sat at the table on the terrace. The moon was full and we could see all the tiled rooftops around us.

Renaldo pointed straight up into the night sky.

"You see those two stars up there?" he asked me. "The big ones that are so close together?"

"They're beautiful," I said.

They were the biggest in the sky and were right next to each other.

"That's you and I," he said.

I told Renaldo I wasn't ready to sleep yet. I was going to get my new suit and go for a swim in the pool. I knew the water would be wonderfully warm.

I went back to the guesthouse and put on the bikini he had bought me at Palm Beach. As I walked back out to the pool, he whistled and told me I was "real sexy."

"You're right, Gina," he said. "You better not wear that suit when my mother is around. It's a real bikini, isn't it?"

I knew he could see everything except my privates.

He started running alongside the pool right after I jumped in.

"I need to get changed," he said.

"You don't need to change," I told him. "Come feel the water."

He stopped at the edge of the pool and I reached up and pulled him in.

"You're the one who's strong," he said.

"Yes, I am," I said. "I'll tell you what. Let's race. Count to three and we'll race. If I win, what do I get?"

"I'm not telling," he said. "It'll be a surprise."

"If you win, I'm not telling either."

He counted to three and shouted, "Go!"

I beat him to the end of the pool.

"How can you swim that fast?" he asked me. "Are you a professional?"

"No, I just wanted to win."

I pulled myself out of the pool, walked around the edge and dived back in. He didn't see me coming underwater and I grabbed his legs and then bit him on his stomach. He screamed for a second.

I hadn't hurt him. He was just shocked.

"That's what happens if I don't find out what surprise I'm going to get for winning. Here's your surprise, by the way."

I got out of the pool again, took off my suit and walked up and down the side of the pool, like a model on a runway, but completely nude.

"You better put your suit back on," he said. "I don't want anyone to see you like that. Somebody could be coming home late."

"Don't worry," said. "Everybody's sleeping."

I kept walking around and finally went and sat down in one of the chairs.

"It feels good to be naked," I said.

He climbed out of the pool, came over to me, took my two arms and pulled me back into the pool with him. He started kissing me and held me tightly.

We started making love in the warm water of the pool.

"I love to be with you," I said to him afterward. "And that was the surprise for you."

The next morning I was lying in bed next to him when he woke up.

"I want to make some reservations," he said. He was on go already.

"Where are we going?" I asked.

"That's going to be your surprise," he said.

He got up and went off to make a few phone calls. I could see it was a beautiful day out.

"Maybe we can go for a walk," I said.

"Not now though. I've got to make a few calls."

I went for a walk by myself. Their house was right on the beach, just north of Miami. I saw one beautiful home after another as I walked up and then back down the beach.

I came back from my walk and went in to take a shower. After I'd finished, I came out and Renaldo had returned.

"We're going to Disneyland," he said.

"Oh, my God! Really?"

"We'll leave this afternoon. We'll get lunch on the way. We don't need to take much. It's just a short hop away. Take a swimming suit. Maybe a dress in case we want to go out to a restaurant."

"When I was little," I said, "I always wanted to go to Disney land, but no one ever took me. Are you sure you want to go there?"

"Oh, yes. We'll go for three or four days. After that we'll come back and spend time with my mom and then we'll decide what we'll do next."

I had always asked my father to take me to Disneyland when we lived in Key West, but he always said he was too busy. He could never go, and all I could do was dream about being there with him, just the two of us, like we had been when I was a little girl growing up when he loved me best of all.

I packed a few things and we left.

We stopped for lunch along the way.

"You know," I said, "your mom is a beautiful woman. And she's funny. She's got a big heart too. I was talking to her this morning and she was nice. She told me all about Cuba. She told me how hard a time she had there. They had to give up everything there and she was hungry and without any food more than once before she left. I told her that different people were given different hardships. We all go through difficulty at one time or another in our lives. We all have to have our trial. Just like Job."

Renaldo hadn't had his trial yet, I didn't think. I hoped I wouldn't be his first trial.

I was dying to tell him about my past, but I knew that I would break his heart if I did.

I couldn't do that. I couldn't hurt him.

I stopped talking and was quiet for a minute.

"The more I see your mom," I said finally, "the more I like her. She's full of emotion, just like you, Renaldo."

"Yeah, sometimes she's too protective of me, though. But she's getting better. I told her I'm thirty-four now. I didn't need her to tell me what to do anymore."

"Do you know what your mother said to me? She said she asked you once what you were going to be when you grew up and you said you wanted to be the president of the Untied States. Everyone made fun of you for that, she said, and later on she felt sorry for you. She realized it wasn't funny at all. It was good. You had big ideas. She told me that when you wanted something, you got it. You were determined in school, she told me, and you were a top student. It was important to her and to your father that you get a good education."

I felt odd. I should have gone to college. No one ever told me that I would have to earn my own money when I grew up and I should go to college for that. So I never did. I never even finished high school. There was no reason to.

I was embarrassed.

Renaldo even spoke perfect English, better than I did.

I told Renaldo that between his mother and his older sisters—he was the only boy in the house—I though he had been spoiled.

"Yes, I was," he said. "But mostly by my father. He bought me a car even before I was sixteen. It's the Mercedes I still keep here at home."

"It looks brand new," I said.

"I've taken care of it. I've been thinking about getting another one, but I don't want to hurt my father by getting rid of this one. Anyway, it's really a car for young people."

"You're young," I said. "You're like a kid, Renaldo."

"No, I am old. I'm thirty-four and you're only twenty-six. I look young, I know. I look like I'm twenty-five. Of course, you look like you're eighteen."

"Men don't ever grow old," I told him. "Only women do. They get old real fast."

It was dark by the time we got to Disneyland, but I could see lights shining all over the city. It was like a huge forest spread out and full of Christmas trees, all lit up.

At the motel a doorman came up to the car and took our suitcases from the trunk and carried them into the front desk. Then another valet carried them up to our room.

I'd never been to a place like that before.

"This place must be costing you and arm and a leg, Renaldo," I whispered to him.

"Well, you're worth it," he told me. "Every penny of it. This is your surprise, remember?"

I gave him a big kiss.

We went up to our room. The bed was huge and it looked so comfortable. Everything in the room looked brand new. It was beautiful.

Renaldo asked me if I wanted anything to eat or drink and I said I just wanted water. He called for room service and ordered mineral water with slices of lemon for us.

I took my shoes off and slipped under the cover on the bed. I told Renaldo maybe I'd close my eyes for a minute or two.

The bed felt so good under my body and after our long ride my back started to relax immediately. In less than ten minutes I was asleep.

When I woke up, I had no idea where I was and I was somehow surprised to discover I was not at home at my grandma's. I turned over and saw Renaldo sleeping next to me. I put my arms around him and went right back to sleep again.

Renaldo must have woken up then too because after a few minutes I felt him turn to face me. He started touching my face and then he pinched my nose. I opened my eyes, but he didn't say anything.

I ran my fingers through his hair. It was thick and felt so rich. I moved my hand down to his face. His skin felt soft.

We were comfortable with each other.

I whispered sweet nothings into his ear and he looked at me.

I moved up and lay on the top of his chest as he began to run his hands through my hair and pull me to him.

"I've never seen anyone who has as much hair as you do, Gina," he said.

He started caressing my back and then the sides of my arms. I put my hands into his shirt and held his chest very tightly to me.

"Do you have a fever?" he asked me. "You feel very, very hot."

"I don't know. I'm always cold," I said, "but at the moment I'm feeling pretty warm."

"Are you all right?"

"Oh, yes, I'm all right," I said.

I put my mouth close to his ear and said, "I love to be with you."

He whispered back to me, "I love to make love to you. I've never had anyone like you."

He caressed my face with his fingers and told me I was so beautiful.

We made love.

"You're the only one who excites me," he said.

We lay in bed late the last day we were there. Renaldo wasn't showing any signs of waking up yet, so I slipped out of bed, got dressed and went out for a walk.

I wanted to think.

I knew Renaldo deserved a better person than I. I wanted to tell him about my past, but I couldn't. I didn't want to break his heart.

If I had done that, I would never have been able to forgive myself.

I was always saying to myself I wish I hadn't done this, I wish I hadn't done that.

I'd tell myself it was still not too late, but I regretted so much that I had done in my past. If there had only been one person out there who had told me that what I was doing was stupid and dangerous and that if I kept it up, my life would be ruined. But there had been no one.

So I just went along and did whatever my friends were doing. I didn't think about anything in the future. I just thought about getting high right then and there.

That was my profession.

I knew I could never live like everybody else was living. Every time I was sober for a while, I'd fall apart and go back to the same old patterns of my life.

I didn't have any willpower.

As I walked along the sidewalks of the neighborhood around our motel, I realized my cheeks were streaked with tears. There was something in my mind that always made me think this way and feel this sad. That's why I needed drugs.

I asked God to help me and told him he was the only one who could help me. I thought he gave me strength, even more than strength sometimes.

Through him I would sometimes be happy for a while, but then I'd get sad again and start drinking. That would be the end.

Now I had Renaldo.

I wasn't drinking. I wasn't doing drugs.

Maybe, with God's help, I could keep it that way.

I went back to our motel room, took off my clothes and slipped back into bed with Renaldo.

I had my arms around his shoulders and I started gently scratching his back. He woke up.

"That feels so good," he said. "You are just like electricity to me. I've gone out with so many girls in the past, yet I've never been able to feel like this before."

"I don't know what you mean," I told him.

"We should stay in bed all day is what I mean," he said.

"No. This is our last day. I want to walk around some more. I don't know when I'll be back. It's taken me so long to get here and I want to enjoy it. I don't want to miss anything." I looked over at the clock. "Do you know what time it is, Renaldo? It's eleven o'clock. I'm hungry!"

"Okay, we should get up," he said.

I hugged him tightly.

"You know, Gina, I'll never forget this trip. I've never been comfortable with any girl, even if I'd know them for a while. We're made for each other."

We finally got out of bed and when he came back out of the bathroom, he asked me, "Do you know what today is?"

"No. What's today?"

"Well, I've made a reservation for us at a very nice restaurant for tonight. It's steaks and roast beef and lobster and stuff. I know you don't like any other kind of food."

I thanked him and told him how happy I was.

We got dressed and he told me he would come with me for a little while, but then he had some things he had to do by himself. He wanted to get some presents to take home for his family. I told him while he did that I was going to get some postcards to send to my family.

We went and had some lunch and as we were leaving the restaurant to go off by ourselves, he handed me a credit card.

"I am going to give you a limit on how much to spend," he said, "but today's your day to go shopping. We might not come back here for a while. So go enjoy yourself, but don't spend more than four figures."

I needed clothes very badly and I went to a number of boutiques and bought some blouses and shoes and even some post cards. I didn't come anywhere near spending four figures.

I was feeling good and I realized I'd stopped thinking about drugs or alcohol. Usually I'd be looking at all the bottles of liquor behind the bar in the restaurants.

Renaldo didn't drink. He didn't smoke. He was a good example for me.

I wasn't going to touch anything.

When I got back to our room, he was there making some phone calls. I decided to go for another walk because our reservations weren't until eight.

I went out and walked around and was just looking at all the people. I did a little more window shopping, but didn't buy anything else. Sometimes I felt a little sad, but overall I knew I was happy because of Renaldo. I walked and walked and then went back to the room for a little rest before we went out.

He asked me to wear the dress he'd bought me in Palm Beach. I did and it was beautiful. I put on a little make up and a little lipstick.

"You look so beautiful," he said and he grabbed me and kissed me.

He asked me what I'd done when I went out and I told him about the people I watched. I said I had sat by the pool for a while, too, and watched all the little kids splashing and playing together in the water.

"I've noticed you always watch the kids. Someday you'll be a very good mother. I can see how much you love children," he said.

My heart started beating quickly and I turned quickly so he couldn't see the tears in my eyes.

"It's almost eight," he said. "Are you ready to go?"

"Yes."

At the restaurant he asked me what I wanted to drink.

"Seven-Up," I said.

"Are you sure?" he asked.

"Yes."

We sat there and he held my hand under the table. He looked happy.

After dinner he reached into his pocket and pulled out a card. He handed it to me and at first I thought it was a regular post card, but it was a small envelope with a card in it.

"Open it," he said. "Happy birthday!"

"Happy birthday?" I said. "Oh, today's my birthday? That's why you kept asking me what today is! You know, I actually forgot. How'd I do that?"

I stood up and walked over and gave him a big hug and a kiss. There were a lot of people in the restaurant and I suddenly realized many of them were watching me. I went and sat back down, blushing.

I thought Renaldo must have gotten my driver's license and read it sometime when I was sleeping.

He must have known what I was thinking because he said, "Your picture on your driver's license looks so different. You had short hair then."

He reached into his pocket and pulled out a little box and handed it to me.

"What's this?" I asked.

"Just open it,' he said.

I untied the red ribbon and unwrapped the shiny silver paper. The box was hinged and I opened it up and saw the ring.

There was a diamond in the middle surrounded by blue sapphires. It was beautiful.

Renaldo asked me to put it on. It fit perfectly.

"How did you know my size?" I asked.

"I got a little thread and I measured your finger while you were sleeping."

"My God! I've never had a ring like this in my whole life!"

He wiped the tears from my cheeks with the tips of his fingers.

"You don't know how happy I am," I told him. "First, I've always wanted to come to Disneyland. And now this. I don't know what else to say."

I got back up again and went around the little table and hugged him as hard as I could. Now I couldn't care if people watched me.

A few minutes later a waiter arrived with a birthday cake for me. I blew out the candles and then heard people clapping. Everyone in the restaurant started singing "Happy Birthday" to me.

I was blushing again and I couldn't look around. I just stared across the table into Renaldo's dark eyes.

I looked down at the ring and I knew how much he cared about me, but I knew I could not be with him for life.

I should never have started going out with him. He was too nice, too good for me, and I could never have his children.

That night we went to bed very late. I had not celebrated my birthday at all for many years. I had never even thought about it. The last time I could remember celebrating my birthday was when I was twelve, at my grandma's house. My aunt was there. My mother wasn't. She said she couldn't make it. I had no idea where my father was.

After that I never wanted to celebrate my birthday.

Chapter Nineteen

When we got back to his house in Miami, there were still a lot of people visiting at the house. His mother's friends had decided to stay for a month, and there was an extra cook and new help in the house that his mother had hired.

His mother just liked to have people around her, and even though she had a lot of hired help, she liked to prepare things herself too. She'd work with the cook and tell him how to prepare the food and how to decorate it too.

The next night the three of us, Renaldo, his mother and I were sitting around the table.

"Are you leaving tomorrow?" his mother asked.

"Yes," I said.

"Why don't you stay for a little while?" she asked me.

"No, I've got to go back up to Connecticut."

She was acting nicely to me, maybe because she knew I was only going to stay one more night and then be on my way.

I noticed how smooth her skin was and I realized I didn't know how old she really was. She seemed ageless.

That night when I went to bed, I told Renaldo I had never enjoyed myself like this in my life.

"Aren't you glad that we finally did get together?" he asked me.

"I'm sorry, Renaldo. I really didn't want to get involved with any man."

"Why?"

"Because sometimes when two people are together, it gets complicated. I didn't want any complications in my life. Now that I've been with you for a while, I'm not sorry. I've loved every minute with you, but my background is not like yours."

"I understand that. Sometimes you're happy. Sometimes you're not happy."

"You know," I said, "I have no direction."

Renaldo was staring at me. I think he felt sorry for me.

Finally he said, "When you get married, you'll stay home with the kids. You won't need to work. Forget your past, whatever it is. I think you can do better for yourself now."

The next morning I got up very early and went for a little walk. I wanted to smell the fresh air along the beach once more before I left.

I was sad, though.

After my walk I went into the kitchen to say good-bye to his mother. I told her I appreciated everything she had done for me.

We chatted a bit.

I was pretty sure that she wanted Renaldo to get married and have children. She told me she wanted grandchildren, but I felt she wanted them from her own background from the way she was talking to me. That's what she really wanted for her son and for herself.

I told her I wasn't interested in settling down yet. I told her my parents had gotten married when they were seventeen and they were divorced before they were forty.

"I'm too young to settle down," I said to her." I don't know what I want to do yet."

I could see she felt much better after I said that. She knew Renaldo and I had no future.

I realized everyone had his own hardship in life. She had had hers, I had mine.

I gave her a hug and thanked her again. She asked me to come back any time I wanted and kissed me good-bye.

Renaldo and I packed his car and just as we left, I looked back at the house.

"I want to get one last, good look at this place," I said to him. "I might not come back here again. At least for a while."

On the drive to the airport I told Renaldo I had called my mom that morning and she had told me that my grandpa was very sick and might not have much time left to live.

"I've got to go directly home from the airport," I said.

When we got out of the terminal at JFK, he escorted me over to a limousine and paid for my trip to Bridgeport.

I was in tears.

"I'll call you," I said.

"Do you want me to come with you?" he asked.

"No. You've got too much to do."

I got home around six o'clock that night. My mom had left a note for me saying she was in the hospital, and I called her there. She said she'd be home in an hour.

When she walked in the front door, she began crying.

I asked what was wrong and she told me my grandfather had died that afternoon.

I started crying, too, and felt sick because I hadn't seen him before he died.

A few days later we buried him. That night I was home and Renaldo called to see how everything was. I told him my grandpa had died.

"I'm so sorry," he said. "Do you need anything?"

"No. Thank you. I'll call you in a few days. Thanks again for everything. I miss you."

"I love you," he said.

I called him back a few days later. He had mailed a check overnight to my mom's house. He was so generous. I had never dreamed that he would do that, but he knew I didn't have much money and he knew I'd need it.

I used the money to catch up my grandma's bills.

I thanked him on the phone and he said he was glad to have helped me. He had sounded more reserved with me, almost formal, the last few days.

"Gina," he said, "I found out today my company is transferring me to Australia. I'm leaving here next week. I thought I was going to be here for some time, but another guy who had traveled a lot got promoted and I'm moving up into his position. I'm single, so they figure I can go."

My heart dropped.

His mother had told me that he traveled a lot and sometimes for long periods, but I had never expected this.

"Gina, I don't know when I'll be back, but you can come with me."

I was silent on the other end of the phone.

"Are you all right, sweetheart?" he asked. "Do you want to come up here?"

I felt nervous and sad. I had just lost my grandpa and now I was losing Renaldo too.

A few days later I went to see Renaldo.

He knew how unhappy I was.

He asked me again to go with him, but I couldn't do it. I couldn't leave my grandma, I said. She was all alone now that my grandpa had died.

I knew that Renaldo loved me very much and I told him that I loved him too.

"You look worried," he said.

"Renaldo, I've gotten used to you," I said. "I don't know what else to say."

"Don't say anything. You know you can come with me."

"I can't leave my grandma," I said, but all the time I had been thinking that now my grandma had become my excuse. I wouldn't have to tell Renaldo I cold never have his children.

"You can always come to Australia later," he said. "I really want you to come with me."

"I'm the only one my grandma is comfortable with, Renaldo, especially now that my grandpa is gone," I said. "She needs me and I don't have the heart to leave. It wouldn't be right."

I started crying. I wanted to be with Renaldo very much and wanted to go with him, but I couldn't.

"I need you," Renaldo said to me. "I don't know when I'll be back here."

"How long do you usually go for?"

"It depends. Sometimes a month, sometimes a year. I don't know yet. It depends how things go there."

My grandma had always told me, "Good things don't last long."

I had already hurt too many people in my life. I didn't want to hurt him, too, because of the way I was. I wasn't normal. I couldn't have children. I couldn't control myself. I could fall apart at any minute. The only thing that ever really calmed me down was drugs, but Renaldo had come close.

It had been almost two years since I had used, but I knew the time was near.

That night I was sitting in Renaldo's hot tub, but as I soaked there, I couldn't stop crying.

Renaldo came in and gave me a kiss. He thought I was crying over losing my grandpa, but I was crying over Renaldo.

"You'll feel better if you get out of the tub. I'll rub your back."

I adored him.

I got out of the tub, dried myself off with a towel and lay down on the bed. Renaldo came in and told me to lie on my stomach. He started rubbing my back with his strong hands and I closed my eyes.

"You know," he said, "your skin is firm, but your body is tight. You're knotted up. Maybe you should take an aspirin."

I couldn't take aspirin because I had such a weak stomach.

As he rubbed my back, I fell asleep. When I woke up, I looked at the clock on my end table and it was two in the morning. Renaldo was lying next to me.

I moved over next to him and pressed up against his back. I put my arms around him, but I couldn't fall back asleep.

I didn't move because I didn't want to wake him up.

Then he turned over and put his arm around me and touched my cheek with his hand. I loved it when he caressed me while he was sleeping.

I'd miss that.

He got up very early the next morning to go to work.

I got up later and started folding all his shirts, gathering all his socks and underwear and putting everything on his bed in neat little piles.

When he got home from work that afternoon, he was pleased and he told me I was wonderful.

"You're something else," he said. He grabbed me and hugged me. "I don't think I can go without you. I'm crazy about you. Maybe I can send for you later."

"Renaldo, I don't know. Just don't think long term. Sometimes when you make plans, they don't go right. Making plans can be a jinx. You'll write me, though, won't you?"

"Sure."

I finished helping him pack.

As he closed the last suitcase, I grabbed a pillow off the bed and handed him the other pillow.

"Let's have a pillow fight," I said, "and whoever wins gets a surprise!"

As he was taking his shoes and his suit off, I started whacking him with my pillow. He grabbed my feet and I fell back on the bed. He got on top of me and started kissing me. I kissed him back.

"You know, Renaldo, I didn't sleep last night."

"I didn't sleep either. Do you want to take a little nap? Then we can stay up late tonight because I'm leaving in the morning."

We lay down on the bed and tried to take a nap. I was exhausted. I was just starting to fall asleep, but I stopped myself and reached over and pinched his nose.

"That's your surprise," I said.

He pulled me over on top of him.

"You know how much I'm going to miss you?" he said.

"Renaldo, I guess this our last time together … for a while, anyway," I said. "You know what my grandma used to tell me? 'Never go out with a handsome man.' That's what I was thinking when I first met you."

"I'm not that kind of guy. If I want someone, I don't look at anyone else."

He started kissing my ear and then we made love.
I was in tears all the while.

The next morning we got up very early and he finished his packing.
"Do you have everything you need?" I asked him.
"No. I need you," was all he said.
A company car came to pick him up and he told me he would drop me off at my mother's on his way to the airport. I got in the back seat with him and he held my hand. I could see his eyes were moist.
When we got to my mom's, he got out and gave me a kiss and a hug.
"Don't forget," he said. "You'll always be in my heart. You take care of yourself, okay?"
He reached into his pocket and handed me an envelope.
"I think this will take care of you for a while," he said. "I'll write you as soon as I get there. Don't cry."
Renaldo knew it was over.
He never wrote me.
I knew he felt it would be easier for both of us that way, but I knew it wouldn't be easy any way.
It was time for drugs again.

Chapter Twenty

I had moved in with an old boyfriend, a drug dealer, and we were selling Special K, a drug so powerful than even he and I were reluctant to take it. We were shooting heroin instead, sometimes with a little bit of cocaine.

One afternoon a man came to the house to buy some Special K. My boyfriend wasn't home. I sold him several hits, but told him not to take the drug right there. He didn't leave, though, but got back in his car, which he'd parked just down the street, and took the drug.

After a couple minutes I looked back out the window of our house and saw he had gotten out of the car and was lying in the street flailing his arms.

A neighbor had already called the police.

When the police got there, he was clutching the rest of the Special K in his hand. The medics arrived, too, and they finally managed to revive him, but he had almost died.

The police asked him where he had gotten the drug, and he pointed to my house. One policemen took the drugs from his hand and walked over to my house. I was still in my pajamas and pretty high myself. I let the cop in and he found another fifteen grams Special K on the kitchen table. I had forgotten to hide it. He took it as evidence too and took me to the police station in my bathrobe.

My boyfriend was never arrested.

When I went to court to be arraigned, the prosecutor presented the judge with the ingredients of the drug. The analysis showed it was a horse tranquilizer mixed with formaldehyde. We had called it Kanivenal or Special K.

The judge asked me in front of the court, "You're selling this drug?!"

"I bought it from someone else," I said. "I didn't know what was inside it." I really had had no idea. It was my boyfriend selling it usually, except for that one day.

I could have gone to jail for eight years, but the judge gave me two years, plus probation.

My first cell mate was Rhea.

Her friends brought her drugs and we took them together in jail. Sometimes when visitors came in they'd bring their baby with them and hide the drugs in the baby's diaper.

So I never had to get off drugs that whole time I was in jail. If anything, there were more drugs in jail than there were on the street. Plus three of my earlier boyfriends kept sending me money while I was in jail, so I always was able to buy drugs.

Rhea was a short little girl. Less than five feet. She was even more mixed up than I was. We'd run into each other once earlier in rehab and now we'd met again in jail.

Every morning when we got up she'd say to me, "Let's have our cigarette together." One morning she was telling me she'd been on the street working as a prostitute—I'd seen her doing that too—and she had stolen money from one of her johns. The next day she had robbed an old lady on the street and her john had seen her.

He turned her in for revenge. She already had a record so when she went to court, the judge sent her to jail for five years.

Rhea had two kids at home and her mother took care of them while she was in jail.

She was actually a funny girl and was always joking. She just couldn't sit still.

One day I went outside for exercise and she stayed in the cell. She'd been telling me over and over the last couple of days that she didn't want to stay in jail for the whole five years. She kept repeating that.

I went outside for a few hours then came in for an AA meeting. She didn't want to go to that either.

When I got back to the cell, I saw her body hanging from the upper bunk by her pajamas. She'd made them into a noose and had hung herself.

I was in shock. I should've known better than to leave her for that long when I knew how she felt. I had been the only one who was keeping her going.

My next cell mate was a lesbian, but I didn't know that at first.

One night we had taken some drugs together and she sat on my bunk right next to me. She started rubbing her hands on my thighs and then touched me all over my body.

"What the hell are you doing?" I asked her.

"This will feel good," she said. "This will make your time pass faster here. You'll like it. Just take a few more downers and you won't remember anything. You'll just like it."

"You're a lesbian, aren't you?"

"Yes."

I went along with her. We started a sexual relationship and it continued on for all the time we were in jail.

It was lonely in jail.

Sometimes all the girls would get together and just talk. Sometimes they'd show us a movie and we'd have soft drinks, but that was okay because we were already on drugs.

While I was there I started talking to one security guard more and more. We became friends.

I ended up having an affair with him, so he brought me everything I needed in jail. He'd bring me candy. He'd bring me drugs. It was nice to have a friend.

After four or five months, my mom came to visit me. We went outside and sat and watched the other inmates walking around. My mom noticed almost everyone there was as young as I.

That day I told my mom it was her sister and her husband who smoked marijuana the first time with me. They always had it in their house.

"You never told me that," she said.

"Where do you think I learned how to smoke? Sometimes they'd give me grass or alcohol and I'd bring it out to the other kids in the neighborhood."

My mom couldn't believe that my aunt and her husband had smoked pot.

I told her that after that all I would do is go to parties and I got heavily into drugs and liquor. I told her my aunt and her husband never warned me about what would happen if I kept taking drugs.

My mom didn't talk to my aunt for a very, very long time after that.

I asked about my grandma and brother. She said they were fine, but they couldn't come with her because it was too long a drive for them.

"You know, mom, I never told you about my older brother. When Jimmy and I were home alone, we had to lock ourselves in his room to protect ourselves from him. One day I thought he was going to break the door down trying to get to us. He is really crazy, just plain crazy. We were afraid of him. Every time you were gone, he would hit us and throw things at us. One day we crawled in our closet and had locked the door, but he got a hatchet and chopped his way through it so he could get to us."

My mother had thought that my father had broken the door, and I had never told her it was her older son who did it. I was afraid my brother would hurt us even more if we told on him.

I told her that my middle brother had tried to protect me as best he could, but he always got the worst of the beatings by doing that. I loved him for trying to protect me even though, year by year, he got crazier and crazier from all the beatings he took. My older brother would beat him, over and over and over again, punching him in the head until the blood streamed from his nose down over his mouth and chin and soaked his shirt red.

By the time I left home, Jimmy never made much sense any more. He had been so gentle to me, though, when we were younger. He was quiet and never bothered anyone. He'd just play by himself with his toys cars and his airplanes. Sometimes we watched TV together. We liked the horror movies, like Dracula and Frankenstein. We'd always try to count all the fingers on the monsters' hands before they got cut off.

I told her that when I got out of jail, I would stay at my grandma's and look for a job. I'd save some money and then get my own apartment.

My mom thought I was going to be in jail for two years without any drugs or liquor. She didn't know the real scene there and I didn't tell her.

"And how are you doing now," I asked my mother. "All three of your kids have been driving you insane, especially me, haven't they?"

"You should have let me die in my oven that day," she said.

"You know, I saved you, but you've never saved me. I used to be so afraid to come around your house because you always threw me out. I don't know why I went to the house that time, that morning. Something told me to go there. Maybe someone upstairs told me. The paramedics said that if I hadn't gotten there right then, you'd have been dead in another ten minutes. I feel sorry for you, mom."

After she left that day, I didn't see her or hear from her for a long time again.

My lesbian friend had gotten out of jail before I did, but once I got out, I didn't communicate with her anymore. I still had a boyfriend on the outside, the guy I had been with when I got busted for the Special K, but I didn't want to see him again.

I hadn't told the police about him because I didn't want us both to go to jail.

Instead I called my guardian angel and asked him if I could stay with him for a little while, just a few weeks, until I could straighten myself out. He said that was fine.

I stayed less than two weeks because I wanted to get out of his way. That man never touched me even though he was good looking. He was smart, too. He was much older than I, and I figured he just needed a friend, but he never interfered with what I was doing.

He'd just say, "Take care of yourself."

When I left, I gave him a hug and kissed him on the cheek. "You're the best," I said.

I called him again a few weeks later and told him how much I had appreciated what he had done. He said anytime.

He was the only one who would just let me be. His love was like I imagined God's love, unconditional, and I realized he seemed to be filled with a kind of grace. When I was around him, I felt like I had a little grace too.

I began telling my grandma about him. She was old fashioned and religious so I had to be careful when I talked to her, but she was a woman, too.

I couldn't talk to my mom. We were too different. When I talked to her, she'd start screaming. At least my grandma would listen.

I told my grandma that most men wanted to go to bed with me and asked her what I should do. That was all they wanted. Should I charge them, I asked. She laughed. She thought I was joking.

"Sure," she said. "Charge them! Men like the way you look. You're a very sexy girl. Your figure is great. Men like your kind of figure."

"But I look old for my age, grandma," I said.

"No, you don't. Girls today grow up fast. It's not like the old days."

She knew how to answer me, whatever I had to say.

I told her that most of the men I had gone out with were not interested in getting serious or in settling down. Of course, I'd hardly ever gone out with any decent guys. I didn't tell her that most all the guys I knew were druggies. Like me, they weren't themselves. Some of them were hardly there at all.

I told my grandma that I thought I would be alone for as long as I lived, but she told me that someday I would find somebody and I'd live happily ever after.

"So where it this man?" I asked her.

"You're still young," she said. "You've still got a way to go to figure this out for yourself. If you want to have a family, it isn't easy. You'll have to work hard. Marriage is nice, but two people have to work hard at it. You have to be a team. I've been doing it all my life, but I met a good man. We were married sixty years."

"You're one of a kind, grandma," I told her.

"I don't think you're going to have a problem finding a nice man," she said. "You're very pretty although sometimes a man doesn't want a beautiful woman for a wife because he will find a mistress for that. Especially a rich man. They either marry someone with an education or they marry someone just like them. They figure that way they'll have no headaches later on."

I loved the way my grandma talked.

I just wished my mother and I could talk together like that. I wondered if deep down my mother loved me. I was her only daughter. Most of the time now I felt sorry for her, but that was probably because I had hurt her so many times.

One day she called me and we went out to lunch by ourselves. We hadn't been together for quite a while.

She knew I had had another abortion before I had gone to jail the last time and she told me I had killed her grandchild. I had hurt her beyond repair, she said, and the hurt would stay with her for many years. She would have kept the baby for me, she said.

But then she said the child would never have been right anyway. It would have grown up just like me or just like my brother and she never wanted to see another child like me or like him again.

She had been drunk a lot, too, she confessed, when she had been pregnant with the three of us, and that was really why my father had finally left.

I was so confused by what she was saying I began to feel dizzy.

"You have to watch yourself," she suddenly said, and even though we hadn't even finished our lunch, but she put a ten dollar bill down on the table and walked out of the restaurant.

I had to hurry to keep up with her.

She never said another word to me in the car, but just dropped me off at my grandma's on her way home.

No wonder I never understood her.

I finally went by to see my guardian angel.

"Where have you been?" he asked. "I haven't seen you for so long."

"I'm sorry," I told him. "I haven't been feeling well. I'm better now. I'm not staying around here long, but I just wanted to say hello. Are you okay?"

"I'm fine," he said. "I knew that even if I hadn't heard from you, you were going to come by one day. I could feel it."

"Sometimes I'm afraid if I talk you, you're just going to worry," I said. "I'm going to go to Florida. I have a friend down there and I'll get a job. I have to save some money to go, so I'll work around here for a few days."

"How much do you need?" he asked me.

"I just want money to get there and to get by for a little while until I get a job."

He went into his bedroom and I could see him going through his drawers looking for some cash. He came out and handed me a stack of bills.

"That's enough for you to get to Florida and live a little while," he said.

I said no, but he stuffed the bills into my pocket and told me it was okay.

"I owe you," I said.

I told my grandma I had to go back to Florida for a while. I'd gotten a job. I hadn't given her any money for a long time, I said, and now look at her. She needed help. My mom couldn't help her. I was the only one.

She said she would cut back on her expenses. She'd done that before. She wanted me to stay with her.

I told her she still wouldn't have enough money. I needed to go to Florida and make some money. I just asked her to pray for me.

I went back to Key West and got a job at a busy restaurant. It served breakfast and lunch and dinner and I worked and worked and I made a lot of tips.

After two weeks I wrote a letter to my grandmother with a money order in it. I told her I was doing well and I felt much better. I was working every day. The next week I sent her more.

She wrote me back and thanked me.

I had a little room by myself. On my days off I went to the beach. I would just lie there in the sun and it felt good. I hadn't felt that good in a long time. My circulation had improved because of the hot weather there. I had gained weight and I had my strength back again. When you're taking drugs, part of why you're not yourself is because your body is acting so differently.

I didn't date. Quite a few guys asked me to go out, but I'd tell them I was busy and I had to work. I had no time to date.

I was working hard trying to straighten myself out. I was by myself a lot and I had mood swings. At the restaurant they'd often ask what was wrong with me. One day I seemed just fine, they'd say, and the next, it looked like I wanted to kill everyone.

One night I was working late at the restaurant. A man came in and he said he'd been there a couple times before and he'd seen me working there. He asked who I was. He said that a pretty girl like me should be making a lot of money.

"Why don't you quit this restaurant and come work with me. You work hard, but you don't have a lot of money in your pocket. If I give you a job, you will have money in your pocket. And you won't have to work all day and night."

"No, thank you," I said. "I'm fine here."

He kept coming back there and he'd beg me to work for him.

Most of the money I made, I sent to my grandma. I only had a few dollars left for myself, but I didn't need much. I didn't even need clothes because I wore a uniform in the restaurant.

But after a couple more weeks the old temptations grabbed me again and I started working for this man. I knew it was drugs.

I met a lot of rich people and a lot of famous people through him, too. They were all buying heroin and cocaine. They didn't smoke grass. Only poor people smoked grass.

I would deliver the drugs. There was another guy who worked for him, too, and sometimes we'd go together on the deliveries.

I was delivering drugs all over Key West in those days and I started to have a good time. There were some nice clubs there and I would go dancing. I'd go by myself, but guys would invite me to dance. I loved to dance, but I'd almost always go home by myself.

One night I left a club and went driving around with the guy I was working with. I wasn't sure where we were going.

We snorted some cocaine after we came out of another disco, but a policeman had been watching us from his car down the street. He watched us get in my friend's car and then he came up to us, knocked on the window and arrested us. He was in plain clothes.

We were taken to the police station and the cop thought we had sold drugs in the disco. We hadn't. We didn't have any drugs in the car. All we had was the little bit left over from what we had sniffed as we were leaving.

The policeman asked where we had gotten the cocaine and we said that someone had sold it to us. We said we didn't know who it was.

They questioned us more. We said we were just visiting. We came from Connecticut and we weren't staying there long.

When the police processed our names, they found out we already had records. We were in trouble. They insisted we were selling drugs. We called our boss, but he wouldn't come and bail us out. He was too afraid.

We went to jail and stayed there for a month.

When I got out of jail, I went looking for the guy who had given me the job, but I couldn't find him. He'd run away. He still owed me money for the last week I had worked for him, but I realized I was never going to see it.

There was only one way I was going to make any money right away. I went to the side of a busy street I knew and sat down by myself on a bench. I put my hand in the air as the first car drove by.

Soon a man picked me up. I asked him if he wanted to "do something" and told him I needed money.

He pulled his fly down and put my hand in his pants. I told him he had to pay me first. He said he'd pay me when I was done. I knew he wasn't going to pay me, so I screamed. He looked scared and let me out of his car. I ran.

After a little while, I came back out to the street, sat on the bench and put my hand up again. Another man stopped, and I could tell he wasn't a bad one. I asked him if he wanted to do something, and he said get in. He was an older guy. I told him he had to pay me first. I needed money to get home.

We had sex in his car and when we were done, he paid me and let me go.

I walked around and stopped another car with my hand. It was a brand new car and the man driving knew what I was doing. He just opened the car door and I got right in. He seemed like a nice guy. He wore a wedding band and he had on a suit and a tie. I didn't think he'd do anything bad to me.

I told him if he wanted something, he had to pay me because I needed money to get home. He asked me where I came from and I told him Connecticut. I could tell neither of us was afraid of the other. He drove me to a motel that was so dark and dingy, I started to get afraid, but I was desperate for the money.

The man said he would spend part of the evening with me and then he had to go home. He'd pay for the room for the whole night, though, so I could sleep there.

Afterward he gave me more money than I had asked for and he said the extra was to help me get home. He asked me if that was enough and I said yes. He left and I went back to bed and slept through the night.

The next morning around eight o'clock I went and got a free coffee and two donuts from the lobby. After I ate, I flagged a taxi and told the driver to bring me to the airport.

I could only afford to fly stand by. I waited all through the morning and then finally, in the middle of the afternoon, I boarded a plane and flew to New York.

I didn't have any plans.

Chapter Twenty-One

I moved back in with some of my old motorcycle gang and started taking all kinds of drugs again, especially heroin and cocaine. Speedballs.

I'd inject myself in between my toes, in the back of my hands, everywhere, until I couldn't find any veins any more.

I started injecting into the backs of my thighs until they became black and blue. It was very painful. I would shoot up over and over again into the backs of my thighs until they were just black and not just black and blue. I thought it would go away. It was only a bruise, I thought.

I was finally in such constant pain there that I started taking prescription drugs, along with the speedballs, to kill the pain.

One day I showed my thighs to my grandma. She took one look at my legs and screamed.

"How could you let yourself go like that? You should get yourself to a doctor. How long has this gone on? I can't drive you to a doctor. Call your mom and she will. No. I'll call your mom because she won't listen to you," grandma said.

Grandma called my mother and she came over and looked at the back of my legs.

She took me to the emergency room at St. Vincent's hospital in Bridgeport the same day.

The doctor told me that they would have to scrape all the skin off my legs because it was infected and dead. He said that if I had waited a few more days, they would have had to amputate at least one of my legs.

After the operation, I was in severe pain and they gave me morphine to ease the discomfort. Even after the worst of the wounds healed, it was still so painful that I did not want to live. I was given transfusions to help me recover.

Finally I called one friend of mine and told him to bring me as many drugs as he could, as often as he could, to ease the pain. He did.

The backs of my thighs looked like they'd been eaten by alligators. All the skin was gone where the doctors had scraped it away in surgery and there were large shallow indentations across the backs of my thighs which have never grown back.

My legs were kept elevated for the first few weeks, until they began to heal, and a nurse came every day to change the bandages.

I couldn't walk and I had to stay in physical therapy for more than a month in order to get retrained to walk. My muscles had become atrophied from not moving them for so long.

I had been in bed for a long time.

One night I picked up the phone and called my guardian angel.

He said he hadn't heard from me for a while. He had started to worry. It was your birthday a few weeks ago, he said, and he still had a birthday card for me because he didn't know where to send it. He said he had thought I was going to stop by.

I told him I'd been in bed for more than a month.

"Why didn't you call me?"

"I didn't want to make you worry, but I'm better now. I had a little surgery."

"I want to come see you," he said. "What's your address?"

A few days later he came to visit me. He brought a dozen roses for me and three different boxes of chocolates and a food basket and lots of other little presents. When the nurse let him into my room, he looked like a little Santa Claus with his arms so full.

He asked me what had happened.

I couldn't tell him. I just said I had a little accident and my blood had clotted.

I opened up the chocolates and said, "Thank you so much. You really know what I like." I smelled the flowers and then asked the nurse to put them into a vase for me.

"How long do you have to stay in bed? You look like you're in pain," he said.

"No, I'm okay now," I said.

He didn't stay long because I think he was nervous, but after that, he called me every day. We became a little closer than we had been before.

My skin started to itch about this time. I would scratch it with my fingernails until it opened up and started bleeding. The doctor said maybe I was allergic to the medication.

My body started aching all over and my bones hurt. Then I couldn't keep my food down and I started throwing up every time I ate.

"You don't look good," the nurse said. "Your skin's yellow and even your eyes are yellow."

I had a blood test and the doctor said I had hepatitis.

By then I was almost delirious with fever.

The doctor called my mother and told her I was very bad off and that I might not make it this time. I apparently had had the hepatitis for a while and no one knew it. He told my mother that not many people survived who had it that bad. He thought I had gotten it from the blood transfusions after the leg surgery.

I thought I had gotten it from my needles.

Different doctors started coming in and checking me out, all specialists.

After ten days I still wasn't improving. My condition hadn't changed.

Finally they found an antibiotic that started to bring the fever down and I slowly started to improve.

I found out afterward from my grandma that my mother had taken out a life insurance policy on me. She told my grandma that as long as I was going to die, she might as well get rich from it. Besides, she didn't have enough money for my funeral.

After I had recovered enough to get out of the hospital, my guardian angel brought me home with him.

He didn't realize what he was getting himself into. He had no experience with drug addicts or alcoholics and he wasn't even sure yet that that's what I was.

He had built his home himself with his partners and was getting ready to sell it. He gave me my own bedroom with its own bath.

I had a Bible by the side of my bed and I read it every night before I went to sleep.

I thought I was in heaven.

I finally opened up to Ryan that I had been doing drugs and abusing alcohol for a long time.

He told me he hadn't really known that. He couldn't tell. He said he had seen my mother around town and that she was a very pretty woman, like me, and when he saw her, he thought that I had not come from a bad background.

He asked what had happened to me.

I told him that after my father had died, I got into drugs and alcohol. I had loved my dad and he had been killed because of me.

I told Ryan I had come from an unstable home. My parents had gotten divorced because my dad couldn't cope with what was going on in the house. He couldn't handle the fact that my brother was so sick. He couldn't handle that I was out on the streets or was living with my grandma or my aunt. I guess he couldn't handle my mother's drinking either.

My dad never warned me about drugs. He moved out instead.

I stopped coming home too and started hanging out on the streets with other kids doing drugs and drinking alcohol.

No one disciplined me and no one loved me. I wasn't myself any longer.

My older brother had abused me, too, I told Ryan. He was crazy and beat both me and Jimmy. My mother was busy working two jobs and trying to pay the bills. She didn't know what was happening.

I didn't understand it when my parents separated. I had thought my father would be together with me forever.

I felt lost.

Then, when my father died, I really fell apart. That's when I started to take cocaine, heroin, you name it. That's when I started going in and out of jail, too.

My dad had left me a little money, but I was hanging out with a motorcycle gang then and I gave the leader a big check from my father's inheritance. He never gave it back.

After that I was in a bad motorcycle accident and I ended up in the hospital for a long time. When I got out, I had no place to go, no one to go to.

I was back in the streets again.

Ryan had been listening to all this and he was in tears. He had had no idea I had been through all that.

"I want to help you," he said. "I'm not going to go anywhere until you get better."

I couldn't believe that he could accept all this about me. Maybe he could accept that I couldn't have kids, too. To me not being able to have kids was like original sin. There was nothing that could be done about it.

Ryan might be the only man, I thought, who would still love me after he found out about that. If so, he was like God.

Over the next few weeks, instead of listening to Ryan, I gave him a hard time. The more he tried to help me, the harder a time I gave him.

I wondered if I had done that to God, too, but I had gotten so used to running around in the streets and taking drugs that the streets had become my home. The drugs and liquor had become my friends.

I kept leaving Ryan and going back to them.

Finally Ryan changed the locks on the doors so I couldn't get out of his house any more. I tried to open the door to leave one night when he was sleeping, but all the doors were locked and I had no keys. I went into the bathroom and forced the window open and climbed out. It took me a while and I cut my hand and fingers on the glass I broke, but finally I managed to pull myself up and jump out.

It was three in the morning and I started walking down to Main Street in Bridgeport. When I got near the center of town, where my friends all hung out, a policeman drove by and then turned around and pulled up next to me.

He said he was going to take me to jail for prostitution. I told him I had just come from home and was walking because I couldn't sleep. I just want to walk, I told him.

He said he'd make a deal with me.

"What?" I asked.

"You know I could lock you up. I've seen your name in the station a lot. If I take you there, you know they'll lock you up. Get in the car."

I got in the car and he started to feel my body.

"Have sex with me," he said, "or I'll take you to the police station."

I had sex with him in the patrol car so I didn't have to go to jail.

Afterward I walked to a friend's apartment in downtown Bridgeport. He sold drugs and I needed drugs then. I stayed there for a few days.

Meanwhile Ryan had been looking all over for me. He found a girl who knew me and knew where I was and she gave him my address.

Suddenly he was knocking on the door of the house I was in. My friend went and answered it.

"Is Gina here?" Ryan asked him.

"Maybe."

Ryan pulled out a gun and pointed it at him.

"You'd better get her out here," he said, "or I'm going to shoot you."

"You're not going to shoot me. I'll call the police and you'll go to jail for a long time."

"Maybe. But if you let Gina go, I won't report you for dealing drugs."

My friend got me and pulled me down the hall to Ryan.

Ryan dragged me out to his car.

I told Ryan that I couldn't sleep and I'd gone out walking and this guy had come and picked me up in the street. I used to work for him selling drugs.

"You wanted drugs, huh?" Ryan asked me.

"Yes."

When we got home, Ryan told me that from then on he would buy me drugs, but he made me promise I would only take a little and only when I needed them really badly.

After that he gave me money, so I wasn't completely broke, and he bought me a second hand car too. It was a beautiful Honda Accord and it looked like it was brand new. When he brought it home and I saw it, I started crying.

"Are you sure this is going to be my car?" I asked him.

"You're never gong to hitchhike or walk the streets again," he said.

The next day I cleaned his house and then I went to the grocery store. I cooked dinner for him when I got home. I don't think he'd had a home cooked meal since he had moved out from his parents. His kitchen looked like it had never been used. Like Christopher he went out to eat every night.

Things had been going well for Ryan's business then and he worked very hard, but he always made time for me. He had gone fishing or hunting with his friends a lot because that had relaxed him, he said, but when I started living with him, that changed. He didn't go hunting anymore. He didn't get together at all with his friends.

Instead he watched me like a hawk. He was like a policeman.

Chapter Twenty-Two

After two more months at Ryan's house, I drove the Honda into Bridgeport one night and left it on the street.

I called Ryan and told him to go get the car. I'd hid the key under the seat for him.

I just wanted to get together with my friends again. They were still doing and selling drugs and I was still more comfortable with that life style. Ryan was too good for me. I was too ashamed of myself to deserve him.

When I called him to get the car, Ryan asked me where I was and when I'd be coming home.

I told him I didn't know.

"Well, take care of yourself," he said. "If you want me to come pick you up, call me." He hung up the phone.

Five days later one of the men I was with got high one night and then got angry with me. He chased me out of the house and into the front yard and started hitting me with his fists. I fought back, but he hit me even harder on my arms and head.

Suddenly Ryan came running up with a baseball bat. He had been sitting in his car down the block spying on me.

The man stopped hitting me and ran away.

Ryan brought me home.

He didn't say anything on the ride home. When we went into his house he asked me if I was hungry. I told him I could make myself something to eat. I went into the kitchen and made coffee. I asked him if he wanted something to eat, but he said he'd just have coffee.

"Gina, I had asked you not to go back out there. I gave you money. I gave you a car. I guess that wasn't enough for you. What more can I do for you? You know, a friend of mine came over the other night. He knew I was having problems. He brought some food with him and we had dinner. He said I'd never looked so unhappy. He knew I had brought 'some girl' home, he said, and he told me you were nothing but trouble. He said I should get rid of you. I've promised you that I would do anything to help you, though."

I could tell Ryan was troubled. He hadn't known how bad an addict, how bad an alcoholic I was.

"Gina," he said, "I care for you more than anything. I don't want much from life, but for the longest time you've been in my heart. I almost got married once and all my friends said I should have, but I told them that girl didn't want to marry me. She wanted something else. When you're not wanted, you don't want to force someone. That's the worst thing to do. Gina, you must straighten yourself out. I can't do it for you. I know it's very difficult for you to change."

I stayed with him for a while after that, but I ended up crashing the Honda into a telephone pole and then, after he got me another car, I ran it into a car in an intersection and demolished them both.

Each time I'd been drinking on the sly again.

"Gina," Ryan told me, "You've cost me a lot of money. My own car insurance I can hardly afford now. I think this is your last chance. You know I've been chasing you and looking for you for a long time, but I am wearing myself out now. I've never lived like this before. This isn't life. Gina, try to forget the past. All we want right now is the future. That will be our life. I know you can't quit completely. Your body needs the drugs, the alcohol. They're like water to you. You must drink water. If not, you'll die of thirst. But can't you do them in moderation, a little at a time, until your body gets used to that amount? Eventually you can eliminate all the drugs from your system. You have to if you want to live. And now you've got somebody who really cares for you, someone who wants you around."

"Who's that?" I asked.

"You're looking at him."

"It's you?"

"Yes. All these years I have cared for you, but I never told you. Now that you're opening up about yourself, I'm opening up too. You know, I've always wanted to live a simple life. Just work and pay the bills. I don't make life complicated. That's what my parents taught me. They were simple people too. They worked hard. They ran away from Castro and they came to America and survived. You can always have what you want, my parents told me. I want you."

He gave me a hug.

"I think we can work together," he said.

"I've already told my grandma about you," I said.

He knew what that meant.

"I'm glad," was all he said.

It was late. He held his hand up to my cheek for a minute, told me good night and went into his bedroom. I said good night, got into my tee shirt and climbed into my own bed.

I felt relief. I lay there in bed and closed my eyes, fell asleep and slept straight through until ten the next morning.

He had gotten up early and when I came out of my bedroom, he was already gone.

I felt lighter than usual.

Normally I had a terrible time getting myself out of bed. My head would be hurting. It wouldn't feel clear. My body felt heavy. I'd stay in bed all day sometimes. I had something that was always bothering me. I wasn't free. The drugs had taken over.

Today I felt different.

I got up quickly and went into the kitchen and made myself some coffee and walked around the house with the cup in my hand, just looking out the windows. I got some cereal after a while and as I sat down at the kitchen table to eat it, I saw a little note.

Ryan had written, "I can't wait to see you when I get home. I'll be there for lunch. We can eat together. Please wait for me. See ya later. Love, Ryan."

I cleaned the whole kitchen and then made the beds. I vacuumed. I dusted. I washed all he windows.

When Ryan came home, he told me, "Gina, I've never seen my house like this. You've been working too hard. You shouldn't do that. You need to rest. But thank you. You know, I knew a long time ago, even though I didn't know you, what you were capable of. I could see a quality in you."

I sat with him at the kitchen table to have lunch and he kept staring at me.

"You know, you're beautiful, too," he said. "I never had the guts to ask you to go out with me when we were working at Friendly's. You remember? I always said you were too young for me. Then I decided you could be my friend. You know, it hurt me all these years every time you were looking for help when you were in trouble. I didn't show it. I knew that you were young and that you wanted to have fun. I wouldn't interfere, no matter what you were doing. I thought that's what friends were for. It wasn't the time then. Now is the time, though."

He kept looking at me.

"You have a scar on your cheek," he said. "You could have plastic surgery and we could fix that."

He leaned over and hugged me.

"Okay," he said. "It's warm out. Put on your jeans and sneaks on then come with me this afternoon."

I got in his truck with him and he drove to a couple shops to get some stuff for the kitchen of the house he was working on. I'd sit in the huge truck while he went into the stores to pick up what he needed.

Finally he said we were going to drive to Easton. He was going to look at a property there.

I started thinking a little differently when I was with him that day. I thought about what he'd said about it being a new me. He was different than any other man I'd known. He never had tried to touch me even though I'd know him for all those years.

While we were driving around, I looked outside and rolled my window down. The air seemed so fresh and the trees so green. I looked back over at Ryan.

This man had a heart as big as God's.

"This is the area I work in," he said. "We're almost in Easton now. It's beautiful here. The houses are all isolated from their neighbors because you have to own two or three acres in order to build a house. My partners and I are building a couple of houses around here. I build them and they sell them."

He had never told me exactly what he did. He only said he'd be busy when he left the house in the morning and I only knew he worked in construction somehow. He never talked a lot. He had kept to himself.

When he did say something, I thought he meant it.

I was getting so thirsty.

"We forgot to bring water," I said.

"There's a store right back there just around the corner," he said and started to turn the truck around.

"You don't have to turn around," I said.

"You're thirsty," he said. "We've got to get some water."

He drove back in the other direction.

"You don't have to do this. We can do it later," I said.

"I'm doing it now."

We drove for ten or fifteen minutes until we reached the convenience store and he got me some pretzels, because I'd gotten hungry by then too, and a large bottle of water.

We turned back around and drove on to Easton and the house that he had built.

Sometimes I just didn't know why he ever bothered with me. I couldn't figure out why he'd pay any attention to me.

Ryan started talking more about what he did. I was happy he'd confide in me.

"We sell a lot of houses around here," he said. "My partners and I started five years ago. This is the fourth house I've built from scratch. I used to buy rundown houses and then renovate them."

"I had thought that was all you did."

"I used to. We just started this five years ago. Before I'd live in the houses I was renovating and remodeling, but I figured it cost more to do it that way. It's better to buy the land and start from scratch. When you're renovating, the materials are more expensive and the workers you have to hire have to be more skilled, so they cost more too. It takes a long time to finish given the profit."

I saw him differently now. I was beginning to feel proud of him even though I told myself I had no right to. I hadn't really paid attention to this man when I'd first met him. I was young then. In fact, I hadn't even been old enough to work. I had lied about my age and said I was seventeen even though I was just fifteen. I always looked so much older.

In those days I didn't really care about anything, let alone him. What did I know about life? What did I know about the future? The future was my next bottle, my next hit.

I asked Ryan if he had ever dated.

"Sure," he said. "I date from time to time."

"Did you ever get married?"

"No, there was never enough time for that. My parents needed me because my mother was sick. I was always running around doing things for them when I wasn't running around doing what I needed to do for myself. I had no time for a serious girlfriend. If I wanted to date, I had to be ready to get involved. I wasn't ready. I wasn't settled. I didn't have a lot of money and I didn't make a lot of money. Plus, I always secretly thought of you. So I dated, but I always felt sorry for the girl. I didn't want to hurt her. It wouldn't have been right to waste her time if we had no future."

The next morning, just as I was waking up, Ryan came into my room and put his hand on my head.

I was sweating. My eyes were all red. My body was shaking.

"You need something," he said. "I know what you need."

He called someone and then went out, but was back home within twenty minutes.

He'd managed to get a little heroin for me. He told me he hated to do that, but he knew that was what my body needed. I lifted my head up from my pillow and snorted up the heroin. He made me stay in bed and then he went to work.

Soon I stopped shaking.

I realized it was as he had said. My body needed that drug. My body was used to it. He was a smart man. He had common sense and he had a good heart.

He wasn't going to give up on me.

Even though he told me he had dated on and off, I realized he had been waiting for me. I didn't want to be a burden to him, though, and I decided that when I got better, I would move away so I wouldn't be any further trouble to him.

I didn't know if I would be able to survive, though, if I didn't have anyone to care about me. Only God cared about me, but even so, I would still be lonely. I'd be right back in drugs again, just like I had been every time before.

This man was putting all his strength into helping me get off drugs and liquor. I didn't know why. I was nothing. I had no job. I had no education.

I heard myself saying those things in my mind and realized I had always said those things about myself. Always.

A few hours later I was still lying in bed. Ryan came home and looked in the bedroom door at me.

"I thought you went to work," I said.

"I did. I told my helper what to do and now I'm back to see how you are doing. Are you all right, Gina? I brought your favorite food, some pancakes and sausage. It's still hot. You've got to eat to get your strength back. I bought you a whole bunch of vitamins too."

"Thank you so much."

I sat up and struggled a bit to get out of bed.

"You don't have to get up,' he said.

"No, I'll get up. I'm okay. I've been worse than this before, believe me. Don't worry. I can always be strong, no matter if I'm down or just sick. I can always force myself to get off the bed."

"I'm going to make you some tea, too, not coffee, okay?" he said.

"Sure."

He made tea and I sat and ate the breakfast he had brought home.

After I finished eating, I started to feel a little dizzy and told him I wanted to lie down a bit. I asked him to come tell me if he was going out. He told me he was just going to stay home and make some soup for us for dinner.

I stayed in bed and listened to him working in the kitchen.

I knew this man was the one for me. My grandma had been right.

I realized he cared for me any way I was.

That night I was getting sick again. I was so addicted that anytime I stopped taking the drug, my body would have the same violent reaction.

The next morning Ryan was sitting in the kitchen with me and telling me it was okay if I took a little bit of heroin at a time.

That was my "medicine" for the moment.

"Just don't overdo it," he said. "Try to do as little as you can at a time. I don't even have any wine here at home, but I'll bring you some liquor. But if you want to quit, you have to do it my way. Little by little. No more."

For the next week he never left my side.

I didn't drink at all. I did smoke a little grass from time to time, but I was weaning myself down off the heroin.

None of my friends, none of my family had ever understood my condition. This man had understood.

He was better than the doctors I had been to. They had always just said, "You have to quit. Right here, right now. Totally."

Only Ryan understood how to handle me.

If only I had been able to hang around with him when I was first starting to take drugs. Instead, I just roamed around in the streets like a wild animal.

I'd catch myself thinking those thoughts and I'd remember what he said. "Don't look back." He was right. I couldn't look back. I had to look to the future. I had to look straight ahead.

He'd tell me I had to look in the right direction, straight ahead, as if I was crossing a narrow bridge. Otherwise I'd fall. If I wavered, he said, I should count from one to ten as many times as I needed to get back to the right frame of mind, back to the "new" me.

"You're the only one who knows what you really need," he'd tell me. "Nobody else knows what's good or what's bad for you. God made us that way. Just watch your step from now on so you don't go back to where you were in the past.

"I know," I said. "I was in the jungle. We were all like animals. Even my leg looks like some animal chewed on it and took all the meat off."

Chapter Twenty-Three

One day several weeks later, after Ryan had started going back to work, I asked him to leave me some money before he left. I told him I was going to go out and get some groceries.

After he left, I took the money and went and bought some heroin. After I snorted it, I started to drive home, but I wasn't alert enough to drive. I ran into another car.

I was too afraid to go home after that, so I went to my grandma's and called Ryan and told him I'd had an accident.

"Where are you?" he asked.

"Grandma's"

"I'll come pick you up."

I thought he was going to be angry, but he was not.

When he got there, I asked him to come in.

My grandma said to him, "I'm so glad to meet you. Do you want a cup of tea?"

"No, thank you. I've got to home and do some work still. Are you coming with me, Gina?"

I had been going to stay with my grandma, but I felt so sorry for him when I looked at his face. I knew I'd done wrong, too.

I went home with him.

Altogether I wrecked five cars that he had bought me.

He almost gave up on me after the fifth car. He told me he didn't want me to go out there and hitch hike around any more. That was why he kept buying me all those cars.

I had been living with him almost a year at that time and I had been keeping off drugs. But then one day I just went out again and back to my old friends and went on a heroin binge that lasted almost three weeks. I undid all the good I had done for myself. Even I didn't know why I did that. Maybe I just wanted to be dead on the streets.

I finally dragged myself back to his house one night and he sat me down in a chair in front of him and told me I had to listen to him.

"You have one more chance," he said. "That's it. I'm not going to continue doing this.

No other man in this world cares about you the way that I do. Without me you would be dead. We both know that. This is the last chance you have. Either you go to rehab and dry out or leave my house now. You've got to decide right now. Not tomorrow or next month. Right now."

He had put all his strength, all his heart into me. He had sold everything he had to help me. He sold his business. His partner had bought him out. He sold his house. He told me he had had spent all his money and he had to sell his house to continue. We had moved into a small condo just before I went on my last heroin binge.

I looked at him and started to cry. I asked him to give me one hour to decide.

"You are the one who has kept me alive," I said. "No one else would bother with me. I don't know what to say. I was wrong."

For the first time, when I told him I was wrong, I felt like I really recognized that I had been wrong. I felt like I finally was able to confess my sin to him.

"I know you really love me and care for me," I said. "No one else, not even my family, has done what you have done for me. Run outside now and get some fresh air and then come back in an hour. I'll have something else to say when you come back."

He looked sad and he was pale.

He went outside. I wondered if he would come back in an hour. I was almost afraid he wouldn't.

In exactly one hour—I looked up at the clock—he came back inside.

"This time I am not going to let you down," I told him.

I got down on my knees in front of him and begged him not to give up on me. Not yet.

"I promise you," I said.

I started to cry and I saw he was in tears too.

When he had gone outside, I told him, I had called a rehab facility.

"Can you give me a ride?" I asked him.

"Sure."

He sat down and I went to pack. He told me I didn't have to bring too many things. He could bring me anything I needed when I wanted it.

I hadn't seen his face that relaxed for a long, long time.

In the hour that I had sat in that chair while he was outside, I had thought about ending my life, but I knew that he might follow me if I did and I didn't want anything to happen to him. I realized that if I didn't have him, I would truly be nothing. I would have no life that way either.

I knew this was the last chance I had.

I went into rehab that day and I knew that when I left, I wanted to be a home-maker for him.

Ryan visited me every day.

One day when he came to visit me, I wanted to go outside and walk around. I asked the nurse if I could get some fresh air and she said yes.

We went out on the grounds for a walk.

I still felt that by confessing to him that I really had been wrong, all my life, I had suddenly stopped being twelve years old. I had suddenly stopped craving drugs. I had stopped being evil.

I had grown up in that one moment with him.

"I don't want you to treat me like you treated me the first time you met me and you said I was too young for you," I said to him. "I have been thinking about this for days. That's not true any more. I'm grown up now. I'm a woman now."

He looked at me kind of funny and I saw he was surprised to hear how I felt. We had known each other for so long, but we had never had an intimate relation-ship.

"After I leave here," I said, "you and I will be different together."

He continued to look at me, but didn't say a thing.

He just took my hand and squeezed it.

I gave him a kiss on the cheek.

"I'm very sorry that I've acted the way I've acted with you," I said to him. "Not only that, but I wrecked a lot of cars too." I laughed, and so did he. "If I can repay you, I will. When I get better, I should find a job."

"You have a job," he told me. "When you come home, that will be your job. You don't have to go out and look for anything else."

Almost every other time I had been in rehab, I had visitors who brought me drugs. That time I had no visitors. Except Ryan.

I didn't want any visitors. I didn't want any drugs.

I had to be strong. I prayed every night before I went to sleep for the strength to beat this thing. I knew I had been living an unreal life. I started to recognize who I was and recognize who was helping me. God and a guardian angel. I could never see that clearly before because of the drugs.

Now, sober, my feelings for Ryan changed. I could see he loved me more than anyone I had ever known. He loved me with or without children.

Now I was determined to put all my strength into Ryan as he had put his into me, and be happy with him forever, just like my grandma had said.

Ryan told me one day, "Whatever you're doing now, you're doing for yourself. This time I can tell it's different. You act differently. You talk differently."

He had seen me so many times when I was high on drugs and liquor and I could hardly even talk then. I would babble and he couldn't understand me. He was always so patient with me. I had never known where that patience came from.

Now I was doing better in rehab and every time I saw him, he was looking better too. When I first went into rehab, he had begun to look old and tired. His hair had gone completely white. He had become fat. He was just worn out.

From me.

But as I did better, so did he. Each day I saw him, he looked better. He even had lost all his extra weight.

I started to tell Ryan I couldn't wait to come home to him so we could do things together. He told me not to rush, though, and he reminded me the last time I had been in rehab, I was there for five months, too, but it didn't work then. Stay a little longer, he said.

He wanted me to get better for good.

He told me that when I was a success and had dried out completely, I could help other people do that too, even if I only ever helped one or two.

I wondered if that was the purpose God had been keeping me alive for.

After I had been in rehab for eleven months, I told Ryan I thought I had enough. I wanted to come home and take care of him.

I told him one day to take a good, long look at this place. He was never going to see it again. Or any other place like it.

I was completely dried out and I was never coming back.

I knew it.

Everything I had done in my past was not me.

This was me. Now. New.

I had renewed myself. I kissed the old Gina good-bye when I left rehab. I took my Bible with me and I continued to read it all the time. I prayed for continuing strength to go through any hardships and I realized I did want to help others get through what I had finally gotten through.

It was just as my guardian angel told me and I saw there was a purpose for all the hardships I'd gone through.

I could finally recognize who I was and I knew that God loved me. I loved God too and I realized I always had, even through all my trials.

When I left rehab that last day with Ryan, my head was lighter and I knew I was free from drugs and liquor. I had energy again. I was free from all that poison.

The next morning, after I had gotten out of rehab, Ryan told me he was going out for some donuts.

"Donuts?" I asked. "You don't eat donuts."

"Well, maybe today I'll eat some donuts. You want some? When I get home, we'll eat and go for a ride. It's a nice day."

An hour later he walked back in the front door and told me to come outside with him.

I went out and saw a brand new red Honda in the driveway.

"It's yours," he said and handed me the keys.

I still haven't crashed it.

I've been dried out for twelve years now.

I'm happy.

When I first met Ryan, he had a lot of money. He had a business. He had a nice home. I spent all his money and crashed all his cars. I drove him crazy for ten years.

Now we don't have a lot of money. We have a small, one bedroom condo and we're happy.

I'm living a normal life now.

I'm good.

Finally.

978-0-595-46847-8
0-595-46847-0

www.ingramcontent.com/pod-product-compliance
Lightning Source LLC
Chambersburg PA
CBHW020415290526
45785CB00002B/577